Roberta Weiner
Aug. 3/62.

30/-

TREASURE SEEKERS
AND BORROWERS

TREASURE SEEKERS
AND BORROWERS

Children's Books in Britain
1900 - 1960

by

MARCUS CROUCH

THE LIBRARY ASSOCIATION
CHAUCER HOUSE, MALET PLACE
LONDON
1962

For
ELEANOR FARJEON

Made and printed in England by
STAPLES PRINTERS LIMITED
at their Rochester, Kent, establishment

CONTENTS

ILLUSTRATIONS

INTRODUCTION

Among the many virtues of F. J. Harvey Darton's *Children's Books in England* is the way in which he relates the books of each age to contemporary social and educational ideas. His book is indeed as much a contribution to social as to literary history. When I ventured to essay this survey of children's books in the twentieth century it was my hope that I could similarly show how enormous changes in social behaviour and the materialist revolution were reflected in the books which the children of each generation read for pleasure.

In the event it has proved difficult to find a close relationship between the children's books of the century and the changes taking place all around their authors and publishers. The references change, it is true; balloon gives place to airplane, jet to rocket, but the space-story of the 'fifties is fundamentally remarkably like the 'Reward' of the First World War. In general, authors have preferred to disregard the accelerated tempo of history. The best have aimed at timelessness, the other-worldliness of Narnia or the past indefinite of *The Hobbit*. Lesser men have applied formulae devised in the early years of the century, or earlier.

For this insensitiveness to the spirit of the age there may be many explanations. One is that in the twentieth century children's books became Big Business. Mrs. Ewing and Mrs. Molesworth had been professional writers, it is true, but most of the writers, good or bad, of the nineteenth century had been amateurs, free to indulge their own interests. In the organised world of twentieth-century publishing there was little room for that kind of amateurism. Books, in order to meet the demands of a known market, have had to conform to certain commercial standards.

The following pages will show that a great many writers have resisted the standardization of the age and have written books which are individual, contemporary and enduring. The half-century which produced Beatrix Potter and Edward Ardizzone, E. Nesbit and Mary Norton, Kipling and Rosemary Sutcliff, may be forgiven a little complacency. Writers like this represent the highest reaches of the century. Children, however, do not confine their reading to the best, any more than do their elders. Their minds are formed by Harry Wharton as well as by Stalky. All is grist to their intellectual mills. It has therefore seemed appropriate to give some consideration here to the 'formula' stories of the century. These books have no literary quality, no originality of invention or point of view. They soon disappear from the publisher's lists, being replaced by others as lacking in creative quality. They are read with the uncritical omnivorousness of childhood. They provide the 'bulk' in a child's reading diet. They have their small part in the development of taste. No student of children's books can afford to ignore them.

CHAPTER I

A CHILD'S BOOKS IN THE 'NINETIES

IN 1900 Arthur Ransome was sixteen. By that time he had no doubt put away childish things (his first book was published four years later) but growing up in the 'nineties he had been able to enjoy the company of many good books. Each new generation is richer than the last, because the enduring books accumulate, but there must have been much to be said for being young in 1900.

There was Alice, after thirty-five years unimpaired by time or by the failure of her creator's inspiration in *Sylvie and Bruno*, and Lear's nonsense and George Macdonald's fine-spun fantasy. There was some good verse: Stevenson's *Garden*, first planted fifteen years before, had recently been refreshed with Charles Robinson's decorations, and for the same publisher (John Lane) and with the same artist Kenneth Grahame had made an appealing selection of the verses of Eugene Field. Both these volumes showed, if reluctantly, the influence of Beardsley. A new edition of *Goblin Market* in 1893 reflected rather the spirit of Morris; Laurence Housman's superb grotesques distressing the poetess who could not believe that she had made her goblins so ugly. Christina Rossetti was happier in *Sing Song*, an enchanting book of nursery verse which Arthur Hughes decorated in his finest manner. Besides these modern poems children still enjoyed the 'original verses' of Jane and Ann Taylor, approaching their centenary and still extraordinarily persistent.

If young Ransome had liked fairy tales (and how could he not?) there were many to choose from: Anderson and Grimm in a generous selection of editions, Asbjörnsen, Nisbet Bain's Russian tales, Joseph Jacobs using the authentic language of Faerie in his English, Celtic and Indian collections, above all the rainbow bookshelf for which Andrew Lang was responsible. There were Kingsley's *Heroes* and Hawthorne's *Wonders*. Then there were the picture-books. The golden age was just over, leaving as its heritage Caldecott's robust rusticity, Kate Greenaway's delicacy and Crane's elegant formalism, their colour miraculously rendered by Edmund Evans. Dicky Doyle was out of a different world, but his fairies continued to give delight.

Then there were stories galore: *Coral Island* and *Vice Versa*, *Robinson Crusoe* and *Pilgrim's Progress* (showing no signs of age), *Uncle Remus*, setting a whole generation alight as it did Stalky and Beetle, and *Uncle Tom's Cabin*, a half-century old and its purpose achieved but still read for its story and its characters, *Black Beauty*, *Tom Brown's Schooldays* and, even, *Eric* and *St. Winifred's*. Parents, at least, succumbed to the charms of *Little Lord Fauntleroy* and let their enthusiasm be reflected in the costume of their unfortunate sons. *Sir Toady Lion* spoke more recognisably the tongue of childhood, and so, from across the Atlantic, did Jo and Beth March. Mrs. Ewing and Mrs. Molesworth touched the tender heart. Children went adventuring with Jim Hawkins and Alan Breck, or rode the New Forest rides with Roundheads on their track. With Henty they found out the roots of Anglo-Saxon valour and empire, with Charlotte Yonge the romance of past ages. They explored the hinterland of that strange country, botanically and zoologically baffling, ruled with most benign justice by Mr. Robinson, formerly of Switzerland. They roamed the skies and the depth of earth and sea with Jules Verne. Children of *avant garde* parents read the delicate fantasies of Laurence Housman and Oscar Wilde's elegant moralities. Some sophisticates looked with the eyes of Olympians at Kenneth Grahame's *Golden Age*.

Young Ransome would have been fortunate if he had met only these books. No doubt he read 'Hesba Stretton' along with Stevenson and 'Elizabeth Wetherell' with Mrs. Molesworth with as little a sense of incongruity as a modern child mixing a diet of Enid Blyton and William Mayne. For this was the age of the cautionary tale and the tear-jerker. Children delighted in the tear-drenched pages of *The Wide Wide World* and the middle-class morality of *Jessica's first prayer* and *Christie's old organ*. Mrs. Trimmer's *Robins*, first published in 1786, was still being reprinted into the twentieth century. *Ministering Children* was quoted, with a kind of gruesome relish, by Oswald Bastable.

For Arthur Ransome and his generation, there was much both good and bad to be had, but for the child of discrimination and, perhaps more important, discriminating parents, the good might well predominate. Perhaps most significant of all, the children's books of the 'nineties looked good. Publishers like John Lane and Macmillan took a pride in physical excellence and commissioned artists of the calibre of Arthur Hughes, Hugh Thomson and Edmund J. Sullivan to do work which no other generation of illustrators has surpassed.

The 'nineties were years of turmoil and change, the years of Wilde and Beardsley, of *Jude the Obscure*. The old century died painfully, under its cover of imperial splendour. It was clear that the new age would bring many changes, among others in the attitude towards children and children's books. These changes were foreshadowed in a series of stories appearing during 1898 in the *Pall Mall* and the *Windsor* magazines and published in book-form in the next year under the title *The Story of the Treasure Seekers*. The author was E. Nesbit.

CHAPTER 2

THE EDWARDIAN AGE

THE golden glow of the Edwardian afternoon did not distract attention from the storm clouds on the horizon. Only perhaps a few Noble Lords, who threw out the Budget of 1909 and found to their surprise that this lost them their cherished veto, failed to realise that great changes were on the way, and that the seeds which were to make twentieth-century England not necessarily better but profoundly different from the nineteenth had already been sown.

The two fundamental factors were materialism and socialism. The motor-car in which Kipling careered about Sussex was a symbol of the former; so too were the airplane in which Bleriot landed on the cliffs of Dover and the experiments in wireless telegraphy conducted by Marconi. Socialism, both with and without a capital S, informed almost all aspects of life, in political activities, militant or Fabian, in trade unionism, in measures for social reform, old age pensions, children's acts and health insurance, in the development of voluntary social experiments like Toynbee Hall. Sir William Harcourt had said as long before as 1894, and in a special context, "we are all socialists now", and to an increasingly large extent this was true of political and social trends of the decade. With all this went an awareness of the growing importance of the common man, for whose needs a new kind of literature was evolved, the journalism of the Harmsworth Press.

E. Nesbit is the key figure of the decade. Although she had written much in Victorian days, she was by intelligence and instinct very much a person of the new age. She had been born into an intellectual, unconventional and not affluent family on the London fringe, had received a scrappy education, partly abroad, had married exuberantly but not quite judiciously, and had been driven by need and by a certain natural improvidence into hack writing. She tried her hand at many different forms, without marked success, before in her search for material she stumbled upon treasure-trove in her memories of childhood. E. Nesbit was a Fabian Socialist not merely through the influences of her brilliant feckless husband Hubert Bland, and she took a keen if erratic interest in all the forward movements of her day. The

Bland's house at Well Hall, huge, haunted, chaotically run, became a rendezvous of progressive writers of all kinds, a place to which, in Wells' words, "one rushed down from town at the weekend to snatch one's bed before anyone else got it!".

E. Nesbit was over forty, and had been a professional writer for fifteen years and a story-teller all her life, when she wrote her first successful book for children. Although she lived until 1924, illness and domestic grief shortened her creative life, and all her best work was done between 1899 and 1911. Within this short span she reshaped the family story, the fantasy and the historical romance so fundamentally that there is scarcely a writer in these fields who does not, directly or indirectly, owe her a debt.

(i) The Family Story

The chronicles of the Bastable family were contained in three volumes [*The Story of the Treasure Seekers*, 1899, *The Would-be-goods*, 1901, and *New Treasure Seekers*, 1904] to which their creator later added a few stories of a less successful kind. An omnibus edition was published in 1928, four years after E. Nesbit's death.

There had been several successful attempts in the nineteenth century to capture the authentic tones of childhood, by Mrs. Molesworth and, notably, by Kipling in *Stalky & Co*. [1899]. E. Nesbit's was the first completely consistent picture of a family, drawn with great affection but without illusions. She was greatly helped by her own device of telling the stories in the voice of Oswald Bastable. This enabled her to dispense once and for all with the 'literary' style which had bedevilled the writing of her predecessors and, indeed, many of her contemporaries. Oswald's is not a naturalistic prose – children are not commonly so fluent and amusing – but it recognises the limitations of vocabulary and reference of an intelligent and spirited child. It is in style, and in particular the subtle cadences of dialogue, that the quality of the Bastable stories is most clearly seen. Only a little less successful is the invention of character; each member of the family has that existence outside the pages of the books which is the mark of characterisation of the highest order. Adult characters are sketched in more lightly, but these too are memorable. Only Father never becomes more than a shadow and this is probably a calculated effect. The pervading humour is a Nesbit characteristic, and so too is the occasional, and moving, touch of seriousness.

Stories so true, so funny, so free of moralising – though based on sound values – were a new experience for children in the first years of the century. E. Nesbit's other naturalistic story of this period – *The Railway Children* – was more conventional, with a plot which harked back to the moral tales of the last century. In the writing, the affectionate interest in the characters, particularly in the railway setting, there were many characteristic Nesbit touches. It was her most competently constructed book, and this in itself sets it aside from the rest of her writings.

With the increase in urban growth came a conscious desire to escape into the country. An attractive expression of this urge was E. V. Lucas's *The Slowcoach* [1910]. This was an early example of a kind of book which was to become extremely popular, the story of holiday adventure. A group of children make a holiday tour by caravan in the Midlands. They visit Stratford-upon-Avon, climb Bredon Hill, have a few modest adventures. *The Slowcoach* is not strong in plot, but its picture of self-reliant children encountering and solving difficulties and its fresh open-air atmosphere anticipated by twenty years the work of Arthur Ransome.

There is rather more of Nesbit, but overlaid with sentimentality, in S. R. Crockett's *Sir Toady Crusoe* [1905]. Crockett, a leader of the 'Kailyard' school with which Barrie was associated and the writer of one novel of enduring appeal, had introduced his child hero eight years earlier in *The Surprising Adventures of Sir Toady Lion*. Toady Lion – this was the nearest he could get to pronouncing the name of his hero Richard Coeur-de-Lion – comes near to being a memorable character, and his adventures are tricked out with all the persuasiveness of the professional novelist.

Sir Toady Lion has failed to survive, except in the memory of those who were brought up on him. *The Secret Garden* is equally a period piece. Indeed, although published in 1911, it looked back to the old century, to the mood and atmosphere of Mrs. Molesworth. *The Secret Garden* has however proved most persistent and enjoys in the second half of the twentieth century a popularity rivalled by few of its contemporaries. This is partly because the author of *Little Lord Fauntleroy* was a master of narrative, partly because she drew on her memories to create a setting for her story which is hauntingly romantic.

The school story, launched by Thomas Hughes in 1857 in order to popularise the educational ideas of Arnold of Rugby, and injected with humour and high spirit by Talbot Baines Reed in the 'eighties, received a new lease of life in Desmond Coke's *The Bending of a Twig* [1908] and in the early stories of P. G. Wodehouse. Both writers, though much concerned to show the formation of character through the discipline of playing field and prefects' room, enlivened their narrative with shrewd and humorous observation. Wodehouse indeed might have settled down as a writer of school stories if the inimitable Psmith in *Mike* [1909] had not broken right out of the restrictions of the convention and set his creator on quite other paths. The tales of Greyfriars, St. Jim's and Rookwood belong more obviously to the world of fantasy although it is unlikely that any male writer who grew up in the first quarter of the century has escaped their influence. The girls' school-story too came into its own at this time in the writings of Angela Brazil, whose *The Fortunes of Philippa* [1906] – based on her mother's life and not in the strictest sense a school-story – marked the beginning of a genre which had its heyday in the 'twenties and still continues, only a little marked by the passage of time. The same year saw the publication of H. A. Vachell's *The Hill*, not a book for children but one which by its great popularity awakened a new interest in childhood. *The Hill* was the first, and not the least successful, of a long line of public-school stories for adults.

(ii) *Fantasy*

The Whitgifts of Romney Marsh, on the authority of Kipling, could see farther into a millstone than most, and that has been a characteristic of English writers for children from Carroll to C. S. Lewis. E. Nesbit had her vision of wonders beyond the imagining of ordinary mortals and of worlds beyond this world; she brought to the writing of fantasy however her own sharp awareness of the everyday world. Her fantasies were often very funny, sometimes frightening, occasionally beautiful, but she never, as a lesser writer does, let the fantasy take charge; her magic was governed by inexorable rules of logic.

The first major book of fantasy by E. Nesbit was *Five Children and It* in 1902, although there had been more than a taste of her quality in *Nine Unlikely Tales* in the previous year. Two sequels – *The Phoenix and the Carpet* [1904] and *The Story of the Amulet* [1906] – followed. *The Enchanted Castle* [1907] marks perhaps the highest flight of this kind. There was a decline in inventiveness in *The Magic City* [1910] and *Wet Magic* [1913]. A charming story: *The Wonderful Garden* [1911] perhaps belongs here although there is only a small supernatural element (if any) in it. In all these E. Nesbit enjoyed the collaboration of H. R. Millar, the most sympathetic and perhaps the most talented of her illustrators.

The three books of the five children are as naturalistic in their treatment of the human characters as are the Bastable stories. The magic in the first two books produces results which are the more comical for taking place in an everyday setting. Robert growing "bigger than the baker's boy" – about three times bigger – the children trying to buy buns with spade guineas in Rochester High Street, are painfully realistic situations, however ridiculous the means by which they have been arrived at. The author's method is to concede one magical property and to follow up the consequences with ruthless consistency. Comedy is achieved too by giving the agents of magic strongly human characteristics. The Psammead, a sand-fairy who reluctantly and with malice aforethought grants the children their daily wish, is arrogant, sometimes malevolent, always complacent; a creation of the very greatest originality and entirely convincing. The Phoenix, vain, susceptible, is only a little less in stature.

As the stories went on they became more serious and lost their initial sparkle, until in *The Story of the Amulet* the magic was more than half serious. There is a sober note too in *The Enchanted Castle*, a virtuoso piece written with imagination and occasional great beauty which nevertheless lacks the fresh charm of the earlier fantasies. E. Nesbit's most brilliant invention in this book is almost too successful. The children, putting on a play, make an audience out of clothes hung on a framework of sticks and umbrellas, with faces of grotesquely painted paper. Through a miscalculated use of magic these 'Ugly-Wuglies' come to life. The episode is horribly convincing and sticks most uncomfortably in the memory.

E. Nesbit's sense of fun and fantasy alike was akin to that of F. Anstey [i.e. Thomas Anstey Guthrie], whose *Vice Versa* [1882] derived its humour from a logical application of a magical formula precisely like Nesbit's in *Five Children and It*. Anstey's best work was done in the old century, but *Only Toys!* [1902] had a Nesbit-like charm accentuated by Millar's illustrations.

The other fantasies among Nesbit's contemporaries followed very different paths. The long, complex, influential history of *Peter Pan* began in 1904. Barrie's play received its first performance in December and the story, in the author's own version entitled *Peter and Wendy* with decorations by F. D. Bedford, appeared seven years later. The curious wayward story *Peter Pan in Kensington Gardens* was published in 1906; this was a highly personal piece of make-believe around and about Kensington Gardens which, apart from Arthur Rackham's

illustrations, is for devotees only. *Peter Pan* itself has become embedded
deep in the national consciousness. No other play has such a continuous
tradition of performance; no other character in a children's book, not
even Alice, is such a household name. It is difficult to approach *Peter
Pan* in a proper mood of critical detachment to discover if it is a major
work of creative imagination or a masterpiece of sentimental whimsy.
Several generations of children, who are not concerned with the
psychological interpretation of symbols, have had no doubt at all; for
them this is a story of high adventure and high spirits.

Like Barrie, Kenneth Grahame has afforded a profitable field of
investigation to the psychiatrist, who has detected all sorts of interesting
evidence in *The Wind in the Willows*. The generations for whom this

book has been the brightest jewel in the English literary crown ignore the dark complexes discovered by Peter Green. *The Wind in the Willows* appeared, without illustrations other than a frontispiece, in 1908. Kenneth Grahame, a Secretary of the Bank of England, had previously enjoyed a *succes d'estime* with two books of elegant reminiscences of childhood, penetrating and written with conscious artistry. *The Wind in the Willows* began, like *Alice*, as an improvised entertainment for a child, his son Alastair. For publication it was expanded and given a fine polish but it kept the episodic form of its origin. The story is untidy in its narrative and perhaps over-long, but it is distinguished by exquisite writing, sharp and colourful characterisation, above all by its evocation of the English countryside. It breathes the very air of the Berkshire Thames. A. A. Milne turned the story into a play in 1929 with the title *Toad of Toad Hall;* this was brilliantly successful but it squeezed the magic out of Grahame's writing, leaving only a funny story about talking animals. With its motor-cars, picnics and country-house parties, even in its paganism, *The Wind in the Willows* is very much a product of Edwardian England, as topical in its way as anything of E. Nesbit's; it is also one of the most timeless of books. Of the illustrated editions the most successful were Ernest H. Shepard's [1931] which gave a pleasantly homely interpretation of Mole and Toad but missed the nature-mysticism in the text, and Arthur Rackham's (originally commissioned by the Limited Editions Club of New York in 1940 and the artist's last work) which included some delightful landscape-painting.

W. H. Hudson's *A Little Boy Lost* [1905] was highly characteristic work. This was a nature-fantasy, beautifully written but bafflingly difficult to understand. The little boy who runs away from home, lives with savages, wild horses and a mysterious and beautiful woman among the mountains, and who finally drifts out to sea on a raft, may have some allegorical or autobiographical significance, but the author provided no clues to his interpretation. The strength of the book – and after half a century it still has power to haunt the imagination – lies in the sharp actuality of the narrative and the strange pervading beauty of atmosphere.

It is difficult to see any topicality in *The Three Mulla-Mulgars*. The genius of Walter de la Mare [1873–1956] in prose and verse had already been recognised by 1910 when his long and mysterious fantasy appeared. Since that date the book has reappeared in several different forms, with illustrations by Dorothy P. Lathrop, J. A. Shepherd and Mildred E.

Eldridge, and, since 1935, with the less evocative, perhaps easier, title of *The Three Royal Monkeys*. It is still a very difficult book, one which has exercised over a few readers a most powerful influence but which has left the majority puzzled and disturbed.

The Three Mulla-Mulgars is an early and outstanding example of the 'Quest' fantasy. Little Nod the Nizza-neela, youngest and most magical of the royal monkeys, travels with his brothers through wild countries and grave dangers in his search for the kingdom of Assasimman, land of Tishnar. It is a superb, though slow, narrative, with many thrilling adventures, strange characters and an exotic scene. Perhaps the most extraordinary quality of the book is the completeness of its invention; characters, scenery, language, mythology, all have been developed in detail. Nothing comparable appeared in children's literature until Professor Tolkien introduced his Hobbit a quarter of a century later. *The Three Mulla-Mulgars* is a sober masterpiece, intensely serious for all its occasional comic episodes, and written in quiet, dignified and sensitive prose which rises occasionally to high eloquence: "There was work to be done, and brave hearts must take courage, else sorrow and trouble would be nothing but evil.".

Of all the great fantasies of the first decade of the century this is the most magical and the most convinced. E. Nesbit, Grahame and Barrie, for all that they may play with magic, are firmly rooted in the real world. De la Mare's story is of a world of his imagining; a world, however, which is more real to him than the everyday world, one moreover which is based in a profound human philosophy. The poet was writing here something not formal or artificial enough to be an allegory; the book might fairly be called an allegorical fantasy embodying fundamental poetical truths. Not, except superficially, a book for children, it is a book in which certain readers, children among them, can discover a luminous, simple wisdom.

(iii) *Discovering the past*

Unlike most fictional families, the Bastables were readers, and critics of what they read. Oswald was outspoken about his contempt for some contemporary writers (unnamed because "I know all about libel actions"), but for one writer he had continuous unstinted praise. This was Kipling, who in turn admired E. Nesbit's books. In one particular the two worked on parallel lines.

Among her many sincere and undisciplined enthusiasms Nesbit had a passion for the past. This she indulged in *The Story of the Amulet* after

talks with Dr. Wallis Budge at the British Museum had set her imagination roaming into the deep past. The Amulet history is imperfectly
digested, but two years later she attempted a historical task which was,
if not more congenial, less ambitious. This was *The House of Arden*
[1908], the first of two stories which illustrated the continuity of history.
It was a fantasy using as magical agent a white mole, Mouldiwarp,
who was in the manner of, but a little less entertaining than, the
Psammead. A rather tiresome boy is proved to be Lord Arden, last of
a noble but impoverished line, and, under the Mouldiwarp's tutelage,
he goes into the past in search of the family fortune and gradually finds
in himself an appropriate nobility of character. The historical scenes are
handled skilfully, but what lingers most in the memory are the magical
transitions from present to past. E. Nesbit did not in this story observe
the fine magical logic of the 'Five Children' stories, but her mastery of
atmosphere was as strong as ever.

The sequel, *Harding's Luck* [1909], is one of the most interesting of
the Nesbit stories. It is the least funny of the major books, but it has a
rare intensity of purpose. Dickie Harding is a penniless waif who has
gone on the road with a tramp; he is also Richard Arden, the rightful
heir to the Arden title who can on occasion take his place in Stuart
England. In her contrasted pictures of life in a noble household and in
the slums of Deptford, E. Nesbit was most consciously the Fabian
socialist, and, if her solution of Dicky's problem is sentimental, she
describes his dilemma in a transparently sincere manner.

In the year of *The Story of the Amulet* Kipling published *Puck of Pook's
Hill*. For E. Nesbit, history was a source of romantic adventure; for
Kipling, it was a key to the problems of the present.

From his earliest days Kipling had known the timeless ways of India
and had breathed in the Eastern doctrines of reincarnation. His conception of the oneness of past and present became reinforced after he settled
in Sussex, in an ancient house and surrounded by evidences of the past
not only in monuments of earth and stone but in the speech and
customs of country folk. *Puck of Pook's Hill* and its sequel *Rewards and
Fairies* [1910] were an attempt to cast in story form his idea of the
continuity of history and his concept of national greatness. His con-
clusions may not now be universally acceptable, but the child who has
come under the spell of these books will never thereafter look with
indifference at the pattern of the English countryside but will see in the
position of fields and trees a clue to the past.

Like E. Nesbit's 'Arden' stories, the 'Puck' stories record a meeting of past and present, although in reverse, for Kipling brings his Roman centurion and Norman knight out of the past to tell their stories to Dan and Una. The device is not fortuitous. It is essential to Kipling's purpose that the children should see time as one, and recognise in the generations of rustic Hobdens and in the unchanging figure of Puck milestones in history and signposts from one age to another. Writing his best prose since *Kim*, Kipling put into the 'Puck' books everything that meant most to him and in his absorption in the task forgot the tiresome stylistic tricks which disfigured some of his work.

Kipling's imperialism was complex, highly individual, often contradictory. Henty's by contrast, was simple as a child's faith in God or Father or Santa Claus. G. A. Henty belonged to the nineteenth century, but his naïve, single-minded, thrilling stories continued to find readers until the beginning of the Second World War. So did the two remarkable romances of the Middle Ages, in their way too an investigation of the origins of British greatness, which meant so much more than Sherlock Holmes to Conan Doyle.

Younger writers were exploring the past. One of the most remarkable historical romances of the time was *Martin Hyde, Duke's Messenger* [1910] with which John Masefield began his long and profitable association with children's literature. This story of the Monmouth Rebellion showed a fine mastery of narrative pace; it was moreover an early example of the 'unofficial' historical treatment of the kind with which Geoffrey Trease became associated in the 'thirties.

To this time belongs the beginning of a series of historical romances not designed for children yet which they quickly, and joyously, adopted as their own. *The Scarlet Pimpernel* was first published in 1905, and in a number of sequels the Baroness Orczy followed the fortunes of her aristocratic and elegant hero. These may scarcely be 'literature' but they have exercised a powerful influence over several generations and their influence is plain in much romantic writing for children right up to Ronald Welch's *Escape from France* in 1960.

(iv) *The cult of nature*

In 1882 *Bevis* had been an isolated phenomenon, the work of a writer who attracted disciples rather than imitators. At the beginning of the twentieth century, however, a reaction against the progressive urbanising and industrialisation of life (a reaction which in another sphere had given birth to the National Trust) produced many books which tried to capture the spirit of wild nature. *Bevis* was published in a new edition in 1904 and enjoyed some success, although it was not until the superb story was matched with Ernest H. Shepard's illustrations in 1932 that it won wide esteem.

A fresh wind blows through much writing of this period, not only in the willows but across the soft hills among which the Slowcoach made its pleasant way; it blows strongly in Alfred Ollivant's memorable story of a working dog, *Owd Bob* [1898]. But the freshest writing about life in the wild came from overseas, in particular from across the Atlantic.

The most immediate effect was made by Jack London, a stormy figure, in his day the angriest of young men, turning from his sociological controversies to point to a way of life which, however hard and ruthless, was governed by laws more satisfactory than those of civilization. Jack London's stories of animals and wild life in the American North were not for children, but it was not long before children had found in them the quality for which they were seeking. *The Call of the Wild* [1903] was perhaps the most characteristic, but *White Fang* [English edition 1907] was more popular and had a great many imitators, of which the closest to the spirit of the original was James Oliver Curwood's *Kazan the Wolf Dog* [1914]. Less complex as a man and a writer was Sir Charles Roberts, whose *The Haunters of the Silences* appeared in 1907, and enjoyed a success which still continues. To this company too belongs *Jock of the Bushveld* [1907], Sir Percy Fitzpatrick's long finely observed story of a dog in the South African wilds which still finds its readers.

Far the most important 'nature' story of this period, however, was Ernest Thompson Seton's *Two Little Savages* [1903]. Seton was English by birth, but went to Canada in childhood. His first stories of animals, roughly contemporary with *The Jungle Book* stories, were more naturalistic than Kipling's and were based on personal experience and observation. All Seton's writing, in fact, was to a large extent autobiographical and *Two Little Savages* (reprinted as recently as 1960) is a classic example of the autobiographical adventure-story. Rather slow in narrative (like *Bevis*), its strength lies not so much in the story, which lacks concentration, as in the handling of episodes and in its authentic detail. Sam and Yan, the two little savages, are resourceful in just the same way as are the Swallows and Amazons, and like them are intensely interested in the technique of living rough. *Two Little Savages*, a milestone on the road to do-it-yourself, foreshadowed to some extent the Boy Scount movement. Eric Linklater's fine appreciation of

Arthur Ransome: "He makes a tale of adventure a handbook to adventure" is as true of Ernest Thompson Seton.

(v) *Adventure*

In *Stalky & Co* Kipling had given a paralyzing blow to the *Eric* and *St. Winifred's* school-story. In *Kim* [1901] he did not so much destroy as ignore the Ballantyne and Kingston tale of adventure. *Stalky* was a joke, albeit a serious one. *Kim* came from the heart's-blood. It is often funny (with the humour which produces the inward glow, not the outward chuckle), but it is entirely serious. Into its writing went all the author's feelings for the British Raj leavened with his understanding of the deeper strength and wisdom of the East. Kim stands between East and West, and is pulled painfully by either side, but the reader can have little doubt where the author's sympathies lie between Creighton Sahib and the lama.

Kim is a secret-service thriller; it is also the story of a quest for Self; perhaps above all it is a story of India, the teeming life flowing along the Grand Trunk Road, the crowded *te-rain*, the lonely truth-revealing hills. It is not a book for children; but children, reading it for its excitement and the untidy splendours of its narrative, have sometimes discovered that a great book may be read simultaneously on several planes, and have captured a little of the meaning of the lama's quest.

Like the Kipling of *Kim*, H. G. Wells was not writing for children, but his eager questioning mind helped many later, and inferior, writers to break the bounds of probability. Certainly children were quick to make his scientific romances their own and to recognise in a book like *The First Men on the Moon* [1901] a first-rate story activated by a fine scientific brain and controlled by a ripe humanitarianism. Jules Verne had anticipated by many years Wells' experiments in scientific fiction, but Wells surpassed him in narrative, in vision, above all in psychology. It is the ordinariness of Wells' settings, the everyday accuracy of his character-drawing, which heightens the effect of his bold technological forecasting; and it is this blending of naturalism and scientific fantasy which brings his books within the grasp of children.

John Buchan's was a very different imagination, but his romances, like Kipling's, were deepened by his strong sense of tradition and of duty. It was the First World War that gave direction to his work, but earlier he showed his quality in *Prester John* [1910], a magnificent yarn which was something more, and which suffered less than most of his later books from a fatal impatience with the working-out of the narrative. *Prester John*, an infinitely slighter work than *Kim*, turns its back just as decisively on the conventions of the boy's adventure-story.

(vi) *Looking back*

It would be rash to read into an interest in the primitive literature of the folk-tale a reaction to urban civilisation similar to that which produced the 'nature' stories of Seton and Jack London. In fact each generation turns back to its origins and recreates the peasant epics and anecdotes of German forests and Scandinavian mountains. Nevertheless in the last years of the old century and the first of the new the passion for folk-tales was informed by a nice blending of scholarship and artistry which had most happy results. The connoisseur of folk-tales was Andrew Lang, whose 'colour' books began in 1889 with *The Blue Fairy Book*. His incomparable series was almost complete by 1900 (although the 'lilac' book appeared as late as 1910), but they dominated every nursery for at least the first quarter of the century. Joseph Jacob's five collections were not much less influential, and editions of Grimm and Asbjörnsen continued to appear. An edition of Grimm decorated by R. Anning Bell marked the beginning, in 1901, of Dent's Young People's Classics. The repertoire of the story-teller grew steadily. A selection of *Hauff's Tales*, translated by Sybil Thesiger, appeared in 1905, and W. H. D. Rouse edited an Indian collection *The Talking Thrush* in 1899. Grace James' Japanese tales *Green Willow* followed in 1910. A memorable book of British tales, to which Ernest Rhys managed to add his personal touch of Celtic magic, was *Fairy Gold* [1906] which for many readers opened new doors of wonder and poetry.

Notable introductions to great literature of the past appeared at this time. Alfred J. Church's prose version of *The Odyssey* appeared in 1906, and *The Iliad* and *The Aeneid* followed in successive years. Before this, some children had seen for the first time the towers of Ilium in Lang, Leaf and Myers' prose of which a revised edition was published in 1903. Mary Macleod introduced children to Shakespeare in *The Shakespeare Story Book* in 1902, with pleasant illustrations by Gordon Browne. Her *Book of King Arthur and His Noble Knights* had come out in 1900. But the finest introduction to Malory came across the Atlantic in 1903. This was Howard Pyle's *The Story of King Arthur and His Knights*, a noble story nobly told and illustrated. Hugh Thomson added exquisite and characteristic illustrations to an edition of Chaucer, *Tales of the Canterbury Pilgrims* in 1904. Harrap's 'Told Through the Ages' series began in 1904, and in 1909 a first attempt was made to show to children the whole perspective of their literary heritage in H. E. Marshall's *English Literature for Boys and Girls*.

(vii) *Words and pictures*

The great age of the English Picture-book was over by 1900, although Edmund Evans continued to work well into the new century and Walter Crane lived until 1915, bringing out such a characteristic work as *A Flower Wedding, Described by Two Wallflowers* in 1905. Kate Greenaway's last work (she died in 1901) was *The April Baby's Book of Tunes* [1900] to a text by Elizabeth von Arnim. The picture-book of the twentieth century was to move in a different direction from that of Caldecott, Greenaway and Crane. A startling indication of things to come was the *Alphabet* which William Nicholson produced for Heinemann's in 1898 – not perhaps a children's book at all, but a landmark in book-design with its strong simplicity and disdain of contemporary aesthetic fussiness.

Caldecott and his peers had found their material in nursery-rhymes, in the verses of the Taylors, and elsewhere. It is not too much to say that the text rarely mattered except as an excuse for the pictures. In the next generation of picture-book artists, the words for the first time assumed equal importance with the pictures. For this shift of emphasis Beatrix Potter was, perhaps unconsciously, responsible.

Beatrix Potter was a self-taught artist of extraordinary range and sensibility. An addiction to pets, conventional and unconventional, had made her familiar with the appearance and habits of a wide variety of animals. In visits to museums and during the perennial peregrinations of her wealthy family from one great house to another, she had learned to render in line and colour the texture of brick and stone, furniture and clothing, and she had an expert's knowledge of trees, flowers and fungi. Her journals, kept in a code which Mr. Leslie Linder has deciphered but not yet published, show her to have had from girlhood a command of vigorous and precise prose. Everything she drew or wrote shows that she had a most penetrating and exact observation of behaviour as well as of physical phenomena. A long secret apprenticeship led to *The Tale of Peter Rabbit* [1901], in which she turned a letter she had once scribbled for the amusement of a child friend into a small masterprice of narrative and art.

Like E. Nesbit, Beatrix Potter did not find herself until middle age and then did all her best work within the space of not much more than a decade. After her marriage in 1913 she wrote little of consequence, devoting herself instead to farming and the management of her considerable Lakeland estates. Between 1901 and 1913 however she produced nineteen little books which for many children have laid the foundations of a lifelong delight in word and line and tone.

The essence of Beatrix Potter's work – it is seen at its best in *The Tailor of Gloucester* and at its most characteristic in *The Roly-Poly Pudding* (later called *The Tale of Samuel Whiskers*) – is observation. She has studied her subject closely and renders it faithfully; she is familiar too with the motives of human behaviour (for her animals, however accurately drawn even when clothed, have human characteristics). Her miniature stories are nearly always constructed with great skill, and she is a master of an indestructible prose style. It would be quite impossible to paraphrase one of her stories, so precise is the use of every word and phrase. The exquisite water-colours place each story in its setting of architecture and landscape, and put the artist, however humbly, in the mainstream of English art.

Beatrix Potter's nearest contemporary in time, and the only artist to challenge her in humour and shrewdness, was L. Leslie Brooke. Brooke, for all the strong individuality of his style, is the heir of Caldecott. He has the master's robust imagination and delight in physical movement. He is kinder, possibly softer; at least Caldecott's equal in technical virtuosity.

Brooke did competent, uncharacteristic illustrations to some of Mrs. Molesworth's books (notably *The Carved Lions* [1895]), before finding his own style in two collections of poems by Edward Lear. *Nonsense Songs* and *The Pelican's Chorus* [1900] showed a ripe appreciation of nonsense allied to practical good sense. This is the quality shown most strongly in *Johnny Crow's Garden* [1903]. Brooke had learnt from his father a ridiculous rhyme about Johnny Crow who made a little garden, in which each animal visitor had a couplet describing his improbable activities. Remembered and augmented, this made perfect material for his exuberant and exact art. He could draw animals supremely well, and he had a rich sense of humour. The result was that the lion, the bear and all Johnny Crow's other friends were depicted with a zoological accuracy which accentuated the incongruity of their actions. This book was so greatly loved that the artist had to produce *Johnny Crow's Party* in 1907, and nearly thirty years later he added *Johnny Crow's New Garden* in the same vein and with all the old sparkle.

Leslie Brooke's drawing is full of movement and dramatic detail. The text is a starting point for all kinds of action and detail which may be latent but are never stated in the words. The lasting success of these books comes partly from their beauty and humour, partly from this richness of texture. Children love to 'read' the pictures, to follow the activities of minor characters in the Johnny Crow books and to study the topographical detail of the three bears' house in *The Golden Goose Book* [1905], a picture-book version of four English fairy-tales which shows him at his most mature. Brooke published very little – he was a 'serious' professional painter – but everything he did shows the hand of a master, firm, precise, with fine technique directed by a keen, kindly eye.

Beatrix Potter's were not the first of the little picture-books which were to become as much a part of nursery life as the enormous picture-folios which could be read only on the floor. Two years before the appearance of *Peter Rabbit*, Helen Bannerman had published *The Story of Little Black Sambo*. Throughout the history of children's literature, books have appeared which have had a success out of all proportion to their artistic merits. *Little Black Sambo*, crudely drawn, unpretentiously written, struck a chord to which children's hearts responded. It was, and is tremendously popular, producing four sequels and a host of imitators. It is difficult to consider *Little Black Sambo* as 'literature', but there can hardly be one children's writer working today whose childhood dreams were not coloured by this absurd, delightful, unforgettable tale.

Other 'little' books followed, from many hands. Characteristic of these, and of its time, is Mrs. Burnett's *Racketty-Packetty House* 'by Queen Crosspatch', with pictures by Harrison Cady, which sheds a pleasant sidelight on the creator of *Little Lord Fauntleroy*.

Peter Rabbit and *Little Black Sambo* endure into the second half of the century, apparently untouched by time. The 'Golliwogg' books which rivalled their popularity in the early days of the century are forgotten. These doggerel verses by Bertha Upton, to which her daughter Florence added pictures of an endearing ugliness, began in 1895 with *The Adventures of Two Dutch Dolls*. A dozen big flat oblong books came out in twelve years and enjoyed a great success, of which Golliwogg himself, lording it in countless households, is the only surviving reminder. Reading them today, it is possible to recapture the vitality, the lively invention, which won these books a reception greater than their intrinsic quality deserved.

The illustrations which Kipling provided for *Just So Stories* [1902] are not much better than Florence Upton's, but they are part of a book which is singularly perfect. These are the stories which Kipling invented for his daughter Elsie, and which had to be told 'just so' with never a change of a word or an inflexion. There is as much wisdom as fun in the tales, which are written in a flexible rhythmic prose exactly matched to each story. The illustrative rhymes and the pictures with their accompanying comments contribute to a minor, but exquisite, work of art.

(viii) *Poetry*

The poetry-loving child was already well supplied by 1900, with Blake's songs, and Watts' hymns, and Lewis Carroll's parodies of Watts and others. Then there were Lear's nonsense rhymes, with their subtle music, and the Taylor sisters and Christina Rossetti. In 1902, however, a book of verses of the most extraordinary originality appeared. This was *Songs of Childhood*, by Walter Ramal (some time was to go by before the author appeared in his own guise as Walter de la Mare). It was not the material which made this so revolutionary a book; in his poems the writer harked back to the world of nursery rhyme, fairy tale and mediaeval romance. It was the intensely personal tone, the technique which seemed so conventional and turned out to be rich in wayward rhythms and odd musical cadences, the effortless virtuosity of the word-play, which put this book in a class apart. In it there was a startling blending of homeliness and remoteness, with strange islands like 'Lone', far off and alien yet described by an eye-witness, and haunting evocations of 'Tartary', and sudden sharp bumpings into everyday life:

> " 'A bumpity ride in a wagon of hay
> For me' says Jane".

De la Mare was one of those writers who are born fully armed. In the succeeding years of a long life he filled in the details of the strange, wonderful land of his inhabiting; but the coastline and the mountains and valleys were all there in *Songs of Childhood*.

Moral rhymes, sometimes gently admonitory, more often savagely retributive, were a feature of the Victorian nursery and probably were carried forward into the Edwardian age. They were blown away for ever in the mighty gust of Hilaire Belloc's *Cautionary Tales for Children* [1908]. The strength of the Cautionary Tales 'designed for the admonition of children between the ages of eight and fourteen years' is that they are so close to their originals in mood and technique. The original poems were not big enough for satire; Belloc's good humoured parody turned them into a kind of art. His exquisitely turned couplets give the ridiculous stories a monumental absurdity which is quite unforgettable.

(ix) *Illustrators*

This was a great age of book-illustration, and one of notable development in book design. The parallel influences of Morris and Beardsley were to be seen, the one in Dent's Illustrated Classics (as in the same publisher's Everyman's Library) and in the elegantly mannered fairy-tales of Laurence Housman, the other in books from the Bodley Head. The latter publisher was one of the earliest to develop a 'House' style.

Some of the major illustrators of the previous age had retired from the scene. Sir John Tenniel lived until 1914, but illustrated no more. His experiences of collaboration with an Oxford Don had cured him of aspirations in that field. Harry Furniss did not die until 1925, but his work belongs to the Victorian age; Arthur Hughes illustrated a few more books, but his best work was done by 1900. But Hugh Thomson continued to decorate books with fine sensibility and unfailing good taste, and H. J. Ford's fantastic humour was, as always, controlled by a sense of design. The most successful black-and-white artist of the decade was perhaps H. R. Millar. Millar had no stylistic tricks, but his work is instantly recognisable for its fine craftsmanship and an unfailing sense of balance. In his use of white space he foreshadowed the work of modern artists like Joan Kiddell-Monroe. He seems to have had with E. Nesbit a kind of intuitive accord which belongs to all successful collaborations; his illustrations to her stories always *illustrate*, that is they give visual forms to the unstated ideas of the author. *The Enchanted Castle* shows him at his best in fantasy, with very fine line and a selection of evocative architectural and scenic detail. His drawings for *Puck of Pook's Hill* are more homely, but they portray character with the simplest and most economical means. Comparison with his contemporary Gordon Browne shows the difference between genius and extreme competence. Browne's Bastable family are pleasantly rendered and he did good work for Anstey and Andrew Lang; his happiest drawing is in the two 'Sir Toady Lion' stories which were well within range of his imagination. Of Nesbit's other illustrators, Spencer Pryse matched her literal humour with his own.

Among established artists who used colour as well as line, the Robinson brothers were prominent. Thomas is the least remembered today, except for his edition of Kingsley's *Heroes* and his share in the Andersen which the three brothers did for Dent's in 1899. Charles had his heyday in the 'nineties with highly decorative illustrations to Oscar Wilde's *Happy Prince, A Child's Garden of Verse* and H. O. Lowry's charming forgotten *Make-Believe*. The youngest brother, William Heath, came to prominence early in the new century. He was the most versatile, turning with ease to severe 'Beardsley' drawings for Edgar Allen Poe, fraily atmospheric Shakespearian water-colours, or the crazily logical mechanical drawings for which he is best remembered. His *Don Quixote* and *Rabelais* were major achievements of their day. The two children's books for which he provided his own text had a gently lunatic charm. *Uncle Lubin* [1902] was beautifully drawn and genially inconsequent. *Bill the Minder*, which followed ten years later, was longer, much more ambitious, and by comparison almost disciplined. It was a book of very real quality.

Many illustrators who were to win high esteem made their appearance at this time, notably Arthur Rackham and Edmund Dulac whose best work belongs to the next two decades. Cecil Aldin's drawings for Walter Emanuel's *Dog Day* [1902] were a promise of things to come, a promise richly fulfilled in 1912 when his edition of *Black Beauty* appeared. Louis Wain's long association with cats began in 1900. Charles Folkard illustrated Grimm in 1911, and interesting work was done by the Brocks (their decorations for the anthology *The Golden Staircase*, still in print, appeared in 1906) and F. D. Bedford. Maxwell Armfield and R. Anning Bell illustrated early volumes in Dent's Illustrated Classics.

CHAPTER 3

IN THE SHADOW OF WAR

It is the idlest speculation to wonder whether the achievements of the first years of the century would have been matched or surpassed if there had been no war. The immediate effect of war was to curtail book-production drastically; its ultimate effects, psychological, social and economic, are virtually incalculable. The war did not prevent the publication of important books, but not until the 'thirties was there in this country a general forward movement in children's books comparable to that of the first decade.

The war was no doubt a contributory reason why the two principal children's authors of the period wrote nothing more of major consequence. Marriage, which offered an opportunity to turn the back on old restrictions, and a growing (and timely) concern with farming, distracted Beatrix Potter from her books, and *The Tale of Pigling Bland* [1913] was her last book in her best manner; domestic griefs and ill-health combined to close the gates of memory for E. Nesbit, and after *The Wonderful Garden* [1911] she sounded only occasionally and briefly her characteristic note.

Many books for children were prompted directly by the war. For almost the first time writers found in the immediate events of the time raw material for stories of adventure – stories, it must be admitted, which only rarely had any documentary value. Most writers were content to apply the old Henty formula to the contemporary events of the Western Front. Three prolific authors who found their inspiration (if the word be not too strong) in the events around them were Brereton, Strang, and Westerman. Captain F. S. Brereton was concerned mainly with the war on land. His *Under Haig in Flanders* [1917] and *With the Allies to the Rhine* [1919] are pseudo-documentary novels which, as the titles suggest, are 'after' Henty; *The Armoured-Car Scouts* [1917], however, is a more unpretentious yarn. Herbert Strang, a most conscientious and energetic writer who exerted a strong influence for at least two decades, wrote stories of greater variety and with an awareness of technological advances in warfare. *The Cruise of the Gyro-Car* [1919] is characteristic. Every front, and all arms, provided material for Percy F. Westerman, whose books are even now not quite forgotten. Naïve characterisation and a rudimentary style were weaknesses for which, in the view of many young readers, great zest in narrative offered ample compensation. *Rounding up the Raider* [1916] is a good example of his work, and *A Lively Bit of the Front* [1918] and *Winning his Wings* [1919] show him finding similar qualities of 'grit' and 'pluck' on land and in the air.

Popular writers for girls also found the war a useful source of material for their stories. Angela Brazil's *A Patriotic Schoolgirl*, in 1918, was a welcome variation on her common theme. In 1918 too Bessie Marchant was to be found thrilling her readers with *A Dangerous Mission; A Tale of Russia in Revolution*, and two years earlier the same writer had covered the Home Front in *A Girl Munition Worker*. It is not difficult to make fun of these books, but Bessie Marchant, it may be remembered, liberated girls' books from their domestic bonds, and took her readers to far countries, to Brazil in *Lois in Charge* [1917] and to the Rockies in *Cynthia Wins* [1918].

War or no war, books in the conventional pattern and emphasising the usual clichés continued to appear. Among writers for boys (and in this period the schism between books for boys and girls became particularly marked) Captain Charles Gilson [*The Pirate Yacht*, 1918] and Andrew Judd [*The Boys of Gunn Island*, 1919] were prominent. Evelyn Everett-Green who had started writing in the nineteenth century, was particularly prolific among girls' authors; it is difficult to distinguish between books written specifically for children and those for simple adults, but *Adventurous Anne* [1916] might be considered typical. Mabel Quiller-Couch's innocent romances – e.g., *A Pair of Red Polls* [1920] – appealed to girls, who also enjoyed the livelier stories, such as *Hollyhock: a Spirit of Mischief* [1916], of L. T. Meade. A book from across the Atlantic, again one on the borderline between children's and adult fiction, breathed an altogether fresher air; this was Gene Stratton-Porter's *A Girl of the Limberlost* which, in a new edition, continues to offer satisfaction to a strangely different generation of girls.

Some years before Bessie Marchant led her breathless readers into revolutionary Russia, a spirit of adventure and sportsmanship had combined with his journalistic work to take Arthur Ransome to the same country. These adventures produced several adult books, but in 1916, fourteen years before the first voyage of 'Swallow' *Old Peter's Russian Tales* appeared. There had been several earlier collections of Russian folk-tales, but none had the freshness, the authentic peasant

quality of this, which preserved the waywardness, the alternation of grim and gay, which gives its individual colour to traditional Russian art. Earlier still, in 1913, Valery Carrick had captured the lighter side of the same folk-art in her *Picture Tales from the Russian*.

It was an age of fairy-tale books, particularly lavishly illustrated editions by Rackham and Dulac with which the austerities of the times were momentarily forgotten, and which, in the 'Gift Books' –

Princess Mary's Gift Book and others – raised funds for worthy wartime causes. Flora A. Steel's *English Fairy Tales* [1918], with Rackham's plates, is typical. In addition to the ordinary edition, there was an *edition de luxe* at the high price of 52s. 6d. Edmund Dulac's *Fairy Book* [1916] was similarly lavish; Rackham's *Allies Fairy Book* [1916] offered an example of the folk-tales of each of the allied nations and an introduction says, a little naïvely, "since we went to press, we have received the good news that Rumania has joined the eight allies. In another edition, we hope to give a specimen of her folk lore, and (who knows?) of that of some other friendly power". F. J. Harvey Darton's more modest *Seven Champions of Christendom* [1914] was a characteristic and topical harking back to the great heroic age. Sir Arthur Quiller-Couch found time from his academic work to retell some of the old tales in elegant fashion in *In Powder and Crinoline* [1918] for which Kay Nielson provided equally mannered plates. From the States came a more worthy rendering of great stories, Padraic Colum's *Adventures of Odysseus and the Tale of Troy* [English edition 1920], a noble prose version of the Iliad and the Odyssey with disturbing decorations by the Hungarian artist Willy Pogany. In the same year this author and artist produced *The King of Ireland's Son* which was only less distinguished. Perhaps the most endearing of the new editions was an *Uncle Remus* with J. A. Shepherd's pictures. This was no *de luxe* book, but an honest and modest tribute by a skilled artist to a homespun masterpiece.

Opportunities for young artists were limited in these difficult times. The most distinguished newcomer was C. Lovat Fraser, who brought to the picture-book a professional sense of style and a leaning towards simplicity which was just this side of preciousness. In 1915 he published an agreeable, well-designed book of *Pirates*, but the best of his early books was his collection of *Nursery Rhymes*, published first by the Poetry Bookshop in 1916 and revised for a new edition by Jack in 1919. In its vivid, flat colours and in the unpretentious boldness of its draughtsmanship, this was the most forward-looking of English picture-books since Nicholson's *Alphabet* in 1898, and like Nicholson's book it had at least half an eye on the adult bookman.

A major development in the presentation of factual material was marked by the publication, in 1918–19, of the first of the Quennells' books, *A History of Everyday Things in England*. The teaching of history, at any rate in books, had always been primarily political and military. The two volumes of Margery and C. H. Quennell's book, however, were concerned with the way that people lived in the past, their daily lives, their homes, their work and their play. Both words and pictures were beautifully simple, with never a line or a word inserted for effect. Mary McGregor's *Story of Rome* [1913] and *Story of Greece* [1914] were in the old tradition in writing and illustration, but there was something enduring in the writer's use of picturesque anecdote and these two books have continued in popularity. In *Letters to Boys* and *Letters to Girls* [1916] Arthur Mee tried to offer a new generation a revised version of the kind of moral and social guidance which had been so prominent a feature of Victorian literature for children.

The most interesting writing, as in almost every other age, was to be found in fantasy. Not all of this was specifically, or even particularly, for children. Algernon Blackwood's *A Princess in Fairyland* [1913], for example, could never have appealed much to the average child; its whimsical humour and sentiment were essentially adult. In *David Blaize and the Blue Door* [1918] E. F. Benson provided a pendant to his stories of David at school and University, showing the wayward logic of the child's imagination. This was a fantasy in the 'Alice' manner which had some charm and humour, but which carried real conviction only in the remarkable episode in which the birds teach David to fly.

In 1919 one of the strangest fantasies of the century appeared. This was *The Treasure of the Isle of Mist*, a story written five years earlier for the amusement of the author's daughter. W. W. Tarn was a classical scholar of repute, later knighted. His home was in Skye, and the Isle of Mist is the true hero of this hauntingly lovely story. The illusive magic of the story is for individual children only, and it has never been popular; but in each generation a few children have found in its gently musical prose and its half-hinted truths the quality which makes for immortality.

One fantasy of the period defies classification. Is *The Crock of Gold* [1913] a book for children? It is certainly, among many other things, a book about childhood. It is full of magic, poetry and farcical humour. If it has not had the impact on children that it deserves, this may be that it has never found the perfect illustrator who might have translated James Stephens' wisdom and fun into definitive visual terms.

Of all writers poets flourish most under the shadow of war. Three of the small band who have made original contributions to the poetry of childhood came to prominence in this period. Walter de la Mare had reached a position of pre-eminence with his first book, and reinforced it with *A Child's Day* [1912] but *Peacock Pie*, in 1913, must have dispelled any surviving doubts about his quality. In its original form, *Peacock Pie* was an unpretentious little book, with plain blue covers and no illustrations. The rhymes had come from various periodical sources, but by some magical process they fused into a perfect book, in which apparently unrelated verses sat side by side as if they had grown there. *Peacock Pie* ranges wide. There are scraps which sound like nursery rhymes, verse stories, word pictures and evocations of atmosphere, in the last section lyrics as frail and subtle as any in literature. These verses are poetry, not poetry for children, but children have ever since taken them for their own, and rightly because Walter de la Mare had described in them a world seen with the candid eyes of a wise child.

Artists have found a challenge in these strong bubbles of verse. The first illustrated edition was Heath Robinson's [1916] which dwelt on the humanity and gentle humour; Claud Lovat Fraser's (drawn as early as 1912) were published in 1924, and used the rhymes as the starting point for independent artistic adventures; Jocelyn Crowe in 1936 provided decorations as fragile and evocative as the verses themselves; Emmet in 1941 offered a topsy-turvy humour; and Ardizzone, five years later, came nearest of all to reconciling the mystical, humorous and homely elements in this inexhaustibly versatile book.

In *Flora* [1919] the poet, with characteristic humility, provided verse 'illustrations' to a set of paintings by a child artist, Pamela Bianco.

Eleanor Farjeon, a lifelong friend of Walter de la Mare, whose work so closely follows and complements his, completed her long self-imposed apprenticeship and published her first book for children in 1916. This was *Nursery Rhymes of London Town*, followed in the next year by *More Nursery Rhymes*. These verses, which provided delightfully improbable explanations of London place-names, were distinguished by a fresh song-like quality which was to be the mark of all this author's work. Unquestionably Eleanor Farjeon "lisped in numbers for the numbers came". She has always written verse with ease, the lines and rhymes tumbling spontaneously from her mind; perhaps for this reason, although she is incapable of a bad poem, only rarely has she touched the deeper note which De la Mare sounded so often. Spontaneity and music are the prevailing qualities of the slighter talent of Rose Fyleman, whose *Fairies and Chimneys* appeared in 1918 and *The Fairy Green* a year later. Perhaps not a poet, Rose Fyleman was a craftsman of distinction, some of whose rhymes have achieved a kind of immortality.

CHAPTER 4

THE YEARS BETWEEN

THE years between 1920 and 1929 witnessed international hopes and disappointments, booms and slumps, industrial unrest and a general strike which brought Britain nearer to revolution than it had been for nearly a century, queer extremes of fashion and social behaviour. Looking back from the standpoint of 1928, the beginning of the century seemed infinitely distant. The whole pattern of life was fundamentally changed.

It is difficult to see much of this reflected in the children's literature of the decade. The mood was, in one way or another, escapist. Most of the best books were fantasies; the general run of popular books dealt with adventures, at home, at school and abroad, which were equally remote from everyday life.

There was a great stimulus to the business of book-making. Many more books were published than ever before. It was the great age of the 'Reward'. Rewards were cheap books, mass-produced from author to binder, designed for the school and Sunday School prize market and to attract the benevolent uncle and aunt at birthday and Christmastide. They were written according to one of several approved formulae, illustrated often with a splendid disregard for subject-matter (the pictures were often reused in different contexts), and printed on an air-filled spongy paper which 'bulked well' (that is, it made the book look longer, and consequently worth more money than in fact it was) but which disintegrated quickly as it was not sufficiently strong to hold the binder's thread. Typical 'Rewards' are noted in the following pages, because they are a considerable and interesting phenomenon of the period; it was, however, virtually impossible for any story of literary or sociological value to be produced in this machine.

'Rewards' were usually written by professional children's authors, who wrote nothing else. Another phenomenon of the time was the number of distinguished writers of adult literature who turned, for the most part briefly, to the writing of children's books. It was as if children's books, which in the 'Reward' trade had reached a new low level, had at the same time become respectable.

38

The 'twenties then were a period of great activity, with a vast output of characterless conventional writing, of some experiment and some achievement, and of an increasing interest in children and their educational and recreative needs.

A self-conscious and systematic concern for children and the books they read had been growing in the United States. Children's libraries there had been in operation for many years, ever since Anne Carroll Moore had 'invented for herself' the position of children's librarian of Brooklyn in 1896. In 1916 the famous Bookshop for Boys and Girls was founded in Boston. Two years later Frederic Melcher, perhaps the most influential man in the world of children's books, became editor of the *Publisher's Weekly*. In 1919 the first appointment in the States of a children's editor was made, to the firm of Macmillan. Melcher instituted the Newbery Medal, for the most distinguished contribution to American literature for children, in 1922, when the first winner was Hendrik Willem van Loon. Two years later Bertha Mahoney founded from her Boston Bookshop The Horn Book Magazine, the first journal in the world to be devoted to the critical appraisal of children's books. American influence led, too, to the founding of *L'Ile Joyeuse*, the children's library in Paris which sprang from the wreckage of the war, with Claire Huchet Bishop as its first librarian.

Although there were many children's departments in public libraries – there had been one at Stepney in 1904, and James Duff Brown had opened one in Islington in 1906 – interest in Britain lagged at least ten years behind America. A characteristic amateurism distinguished most of the best writing for children, and the publishers' attitude was capricious. It may or may not have been a bad thing that children's books in Britain had a further ten years' holiday before professionalism and earnestness caught up with them; certainly the 'twenties were a time of shots in the dark.

(i) *Tradition*

Of the 'twenties, more than of most periods, it would be unsound to judge the literary climate by the books which have survived to the present day. The dozen or so enduring works are overwhelmingly outweighed numerically by floods of books from the popular publishers, some of which have a spark of originality, but most follow a predictable pattern.

To judge from the number of reprints, this was the age of Ballantyne, Henty, Kingston and Rider Haggard and, among girls' writers,

Louisa M. Alcott. There were many series, including Nelson's White Star Series and Herbert Strang's English Library, designed largely to present new editions of the Victorian adventure stories.

New adventure stories drew on the events, and the mythology, of the late War for much of their material. In this field the Westermans, Percy and John, were pre-eminent, although Tom Bevan exceeded them in output. Historical romances were astonishingly popular. Many of Colonel Brereton's were of this kind, but by far the largest number came from the phenomenally prolific Herbert Strang. Titles to his credit, including reprints, fell not far short of one hundred in ten years. Many of these were, perhaps not surprisingly, of little interest. *On London River* [1929] had quality, however; and *Humphrey Bold* [1921], with its splendid sub-title "his chance and mischance by land and sea: a story of the time of Benbow", was better still, with a lively narrative and some authentic atmosphere. Harry Collingwood took readily to every kind of improbable adventure, and outreached most modern writers of science-fiction in *The Cruise of the 'Flying-Ship', the Airship-Submarine* [1924]. Two writers, while content to follow the conventional pattern of the adventure story, showed an unconventional respect for authentic settings and convincing episodes; L. Patrick Greene wrote with pace and honesty, while Laurence R. Bourne in his 'Coppernob' tales [*Coppernob Buckland*, 1925] and still more in *Well Tackled: a Story of a Shipyard* [1928] anticipated to some small extent the 'career' story in his concern for the details of everyday life.

Scouts and guides provided both the subject-matter and the market for a large number of books. B.P. himself was content to write practical handbooks, but many writers used scouting lore as the background to stories of adventure which bore a striking resemblance to those of authors who remained untouched by Baden Powell's great idea. Hayden Dimmock, John Finnemore and Major Clifton-Shelton were prominent among 'scouting' authors, and Vera Barclay, Winifred Darch, Nancy Hayes and, more particularly, Mrs. Osborn Hann, dealt with the activities of Guides. The last-named was the most faithful to her material, and an additional touch of authenticity was added to her stories by the naïvely posed photographic illustrations of real guides and brownies at their work. *Peg's Patrol* [1924] was a typical example of her simple, sincere writing.

The 'twenties were, above all, the age of the school story. There were no significant developments; the boys' story followed the pattern established by T. B. Reed forty years earlier, while hardly anything in the girls' story had escaped the prior attentions of Angela Brazil. In sheer numbers, however, the 'twenties surpassed any previous enterprise of this kind. Among boys' writers Richard Bird, Harold Avery, who had been writing since the beginning of the century, R. A. H. Goodyear [*Forge of Foxenby*, 1920] and Herbert Hayens, with an almost interminable series of 'Play Up!' tales, were particularly active. By far the best of the prolific writers of boys' stories were Gunby Hadath and Hylton Cleaver. Both saw school-life as an excuse to play games, but they described sport (particularly rugby football) with understanding detail and great gusto, and they allowed themselves to show some understanding of the development of character. Cleaver's *Harley First XV* [1922] was typical, as was Gunby Hadath's *Carey of Cobhouse* [1928], although this writer did his best work during the next decade. The traditional girls' school story was represented by Angela Brazil's *Bosom Friends* [1923], a large number of books by Christine Chaundler, the Abbey School books of Elsie Oxenham [*The Abbey Girls*, 1920], May Baldwin's improbably-titled *Girls' Eton* [1929], and Ethel Talbot's *Spirit of the School* and many others. The indefatigable Evelyn Everett Green and May Wynne, both with well over fifty books (including reprints) in the 'twenties, turned indifferently to school, adventure, romance and history for their stories. Three writers explored the convention of school life, and the minds of their heroines, with greater subtlety. Elinor Brent-Dyer's 'Chalet' school stories [*The School at the Chalet*, 1925], and still more Dorita Fairlie Bruce's 'Nancy' and 'Dimsie' books showed a little of the influence not of the traditional school-story but of the 'adult' school novels of Hugh Walpole and others, and this was even more true of Josephine Elder's *Evelyn Finds Herself* [1929] which, for all its conventional structure, showed considerable understanding of child behaviour. Such books stand out so brightly from the grey mass of school-stories that it is tempting to exaggerate their excellences. They are in fact the shallowest of steps towards Elfrida Vipont, but at least they lead upwards.

(ii) *Experiment*

The touchstone of the 'twenties was *Joy Street*. This incomparable annual, with its pendant monthly *Merry-Go-Round*, was a product of the enterprise of Basil Blackwell who played the part almost of Fairy-Godfather throughout the decade.

Joy Street was a meeting-place for literally all the best writing for children. *Number One Joy Street* was written by Walter de la Mare,

Eleanor Farjeon, Belloc, Madeline Nightingale, Kathleen Pyke, Laurence Housman, Mabel Marlowe, Halliwell Sutcliffe, Edith Sitwell, Hugh Chesterman and Rose Fyleman, and the principal illustrator was Alec Buckels. In later numbers, Chesterton, Milne, Walpole, Compton Mackenzie, Lord Dunsany, Algernon Blackwood and others joined the distinguished company. The first story of all after Rose Fyleman's charming introductory poem, began: " When Tom Cobble of Short-ways was seven years old, he got stolen by the fairies" – deathless words to be incorporated in due course into *Martin Pippin in the Daisy Field;* and other stories were later to find their way into Walter de la Mare's collected volumes. Blackwell later took to turning individual stories (or pairs of stories) into little flat books which became a familiar feature of many nurseries of the time. De la Mare's *Miss Jemima*, issued by Blackwell in 1929 at one shilling, was a typical example.

There was a strong emphasis in *Joy Street* on poetic fantasy, and this is maintained in most creative writing of the period. Little attempt was made to write for older children, or to take material from everyday life, and in consequence there were few new books by distinguished writers to compete with the mass-productions of the 'Reward' industry.

Among picture-books, Cecil Aldin did perhaps his most popular work in *Bunnyborough* [1919]. There was a charming Leslie Brooke to a text by R. H. Charles [*A Roundabout Turn*, 1930], and a very character-istic example of Lovat Fraser's elegant manner in *The Luck of the Beanrows* [1921]. For many of the smallest children hardly any books (even Beatrix Potter's) were so dearly loved as the 'Mr.' and 'Mrs.' books of Lawson Wood, highly indurable and not much better artistically than the Upton's 'Golliwoggs' but having for that genera-tion an irresistible, inexplicable appeal.

The most interesting artist of the period was William Nicholson (the former Beggarstaff Brother), now a major artist and tempted into children's books by his own family. As early as 1922 he did enchanting drawings for Margery Williams Bianco's *Velveteen Rabbit*, but his lasting claim to the affection of children depends on *Clever Bill* [1926] and *The Pirate Twins* [1929]. The genesis of these books is described in Marguerite Steen's biography of the artist [Collins, 1943]. The books were written for his daughter Liza (by his second marriage) and for his elder daughter Nancy's children. "Nancy designed the first pirate twin, who was made out of an old sock, and he 'modelled' for his own portrait and that of his brother". The two books show the informality of their origin, but the effortless craftsmanship and the simple perfection of the few words (150 in *Clever Bill*) put them into the front rank among picture-books of the century.

In 1923 appeared the first of a long series of books which were to give much pleasure. This was *The Black Cats and the Tinker's Wife*, in which Margaret and Mary Baker matched a gentle amusing story with most accomplished pictures in black silhouette. This was followed by *The Little Girl Who Curtsied to the Owl* [1925], and the series ended only in 1947.

The Beatrix Potter books continued to exact the homage, not only of children and their parents, but of makers of picture-books for the very young. There is a little of Beatrix Potter, but none of the magic, in Ernest Aris's many books (in the 'Betsy Trot' series and others). The debt was even clearer in a little book which appeared in 1929 and was destined for a long life and many offspring. This was *The Squirrel, the Hare, and the Little Grey Rabbit*, in which Alison Uttley introduced her best-loved characters. In this and in the many succeeding volumes – they still continue – there is insufficient technical ability in Margaret Tempest's illustrations, but the stories, told very simply but with a real sense of style, are enriched with much country lore and, even when they are superficially sentimental, nearly always ring true.

Several of the most memorable characters in children's literature made their first appearance at this time. *The Seven Voyages of Sinbad the Sailor* [1926] had introduced a talented new artist, S. G. Hulme Beaman, and two years later he wrote the first of his 'Toytown' books – *Tales of Toytown*. This enjoyed a modest success, but it was the brilliantly skilful radio presentation that brought wide fame and won deep affection for Larry the Lamb and his friends. Like Worzel Gummidge and Jennings, Larry the Lamb owes more to radio technique than to literary quality for his extraordinary success. The most fantastic success of the decade belonged to A. A. Milne. *When We Were Very Young* in 1924 and *Now We are Six* in 1927 became books that defied criticism. 'Beachcomber' might write biting parodies about 'Christopher Robin falling down stairs"; these touched the books no more than Geoffrey Grigson's more recent scorn. It is possible to point to Milne's metrical facility and verbal wit, as well as to the exquisite aptness of E. H. Shepard's illustrations; these contributed to the success, but they do not explain why children for whom Carroll's richer wit and craftsmanship and Grahame's deeper sensitivity mean little know 'The King's Breakfast' by heart and are deeply involved in the disreputable exploits of Sir Brian Botany. Is it just that the poems are simple and the emotions superficial, or do they speak to something elemental in every child?

Milne matched his success in verse with an equal achievement in *Winnie the Pooh* [1926] and its sequel *The House at Pooh Corner* [1928]. Pooh had already made his appearance in the Christopher Robin verses, but in prose he grew to greater stature (and girth). The stories began, rather uncertainly, as a kind of private family joke, but Pooh, like all really original characters, took charge and lifted the writing onto a different plane, winning for himself as he did so a small but undeniable immortality.

In 1929 Milne made a play – *Toad of Toad Hall* – out of *The Wind in the Willows*. There is more of Milne than Grahame in the play, and to some extent he did injury to the original book by the mere fact of his own success, but, however far from the spirit of *The Wind in the Willows*, *Toad of Toad Hall* was, and remained, one of the few really satisfactory plays for children.

Between 1924 and 1929 Milne won for himself a place in children's literature beside writers who were by any literary standards his superiors. He never succeeded again in recapturing the mood of these books. With the departure of Christopher Robin to school (where he was to rue his father's success) the impulse to write was removed.

Pooh's portly bulk has overshadowed some pleasant and worthy books. Margery Bianco's *Velveteen Rabbit* (already mentioned) and her *Poor Cecco* [1925], a nice story of a wooden dog for which Rackham provided the illustrations, do not deserve their present oblivion. Algernon Blackwood's *Dudley and Gilderoy* [1929] has enjoyed revival on the radio, but this 'nonsense' was given a new lease of life in the edition with Rojankovsky's drawings published in 1941. On a lower level of invention, Esther Boumphrey's *The Hoojibahs* [1929] had an agreeable lunacy which was maintained in a sequel twenty years later. Bernard and Elinor Darwin created a gentle and lovable hero in Mr. Tootleoo, who appeared in two books published by the Nonesuch Press – *The Tale of Mr. Tootleoo* [1926] and *Tootleoo Two* [1927] – and gathered together in 1933.

This was a period of fairy tales, real and artificial. There were no major collections of folk-tales nicely balancing scholarship and entertainment, although in three volumes Romer Wilson found a satisfactory up-to-date addition to Andrew Lang's 'colour' books. *Green Magic*, the first of these, drew on a variety of sources, traditional and literary, and the editor, the wife of Edward J. O'Brien, well-known for his annual collections of short stories, was notable for the respect which she showed for her texts. There was none of the softening which disfigured many collections of the period. At the opposite extreme was Walter de la Mare, who, in *Told Again* [1927], retold some of the most famous of traditional tales, decorating them with all the rich resources of his art. Any other writer must have destroyed the essence of these stories with details out of the spirit of the original; De la Mare's versions seek out and release all kinds of latent possibilities in the familiar tales. The book is a delight in itself and also a handbook to the methods of a master craftsman.

The fairy tales of Hans Andersen continued to exercise their unique power. Between 1921 and 1925 no less than thirty-four editions were published, with a wide range of quality and for a variety of pockets. Among the illustrators were Mabel Lucy Attwell (then at the height of her popularity and matching her slight agreeable talents to *Peter Pan* and *Alice*), Heath Robinson, and Kay Nielson, the last in the handsome 'gift book' manner at a pound, with a 'de luxe' alternative at three guineas. The most competent edition, however, and a major landmark in the understanding of Andersen's true quality was the *Forty Stories* published by Faber in 1930. For this edition M. R. James, Provost of Eton and master ghost-story teller, went to the Danish original and produced a translation which escaped from the stodgy 'literary' English of the conventional versions and found a satisfactory equivalent to Andersen's colloquial style.

There was a spate of original stories in the folk-tale manner. Laurence Housman's beautifully artful tales, mostly published originally at the end of the last century were reissued with new illustrations, in a new format, and a new generation of admirers delighted in *Moonshine and Clover* [1924] and *Turn Again Tales* [1930]. Stephen Southwold (Neil Bell) was another popular writer of short stories in a vein of fantasy, with *In Between Tales* [1923] for which H. R. Millar drew illustrations, and several other collections. There was a stronger element of comedy in Mabel Marlowe's stories *The Wiggly Weasel* [1924] and others. Other short stories were by Rose Fyleman, Susan Buchan, and Cyril Beaumont (the last published by the author in elegant style, with pictures by Wyndham Payne which in retrospect are seen as perfect period pieces). The finest and most enduring of the original stories are gathered together in *Broomsticks* [1925], the first of De la Mare's major collections of short stories. This had decorations by Bold which were as characteristic of the 'twenties as Rex Whistler's for *The Lord Fish* [1933] were of the 'thirties. The stories in *Broomsticks* ranged over a variety of subjects; all had that touch of dream-like melancholy which was the hall-mark of this poet's work in all forms. This is not to say that the stories were uniformly sad. The title-story about a respectable tom cat who joined the witches, is both sinister and funny, and 'The Three Sleeping Boys of Warwickshire' reads like authentic history – if history were ever so perfect in symmetry, so tender and tough.

Three other essays in fantasy may be considered here, one an interesting oddity, the others works of major genius. The oddity was Compton Mackenzie's *Santa Claus in Summer* which appeared in 1924. (It was re-issued in 1960). This was a technical *tour-de-force* which spun into one narrative all the characters from nursery rhymes. The ingenuity of the author wins admiration as much as his high spirits and sense of humour, but it seems an exercise rather than a piece of creative writing. *The Story of Doctor Dolittle* [1920, English edition 1922] is a creative work of nearly the highest order. *Doctor Dolittle* was a product of the war. Hugh Lofting, an Englishman who had gone to live in America in early manhood, returned home to join the Army in 1916. In the trenches he found little to enliven his letters to his children at home, but he became deeply interested in the part that animals, particularly horses, were playing in the war. It seemed unfair that, when they were wounded, their loyalty was repaid with a bullet. Why were there no horse surgeons? Presumably because no doctor could speak horse language. Out of this thought came story-letters about Doctor Dolittle of Puddleby-in-the-Marsh, who gave up his human practice to devote himself to animals and who taught himself even the language of fishes. It was one of the very few entirely original ideas in children's books. The first book about the immortal Doctor was published in America in 1920, and a long stream of them continued to flow until the author's death in 1947. In the course of the years a whole mythology was developed around Doctor Dolittle and, at any rate in the later books, a considerable demand was made on the reader's memory. It might be said that the Doctor Dolittle books are better in conception than in execution; the narrative is often slow, but the stories are illumined by so fine a blend of humour and humanitarianism that they have won generations of devotees in spite of their obvious defects. The intensely serious fun, the consistency, the fundamental sanity of these books, (for the fantasy lies only in the basic idea, not in the working-out) all make a direct and enduring appeal to children.

While the fantasy of *Doctor Dolittle* consists only in the ability of the doctor to communicate with animals and in the existence of creatures like the Pushmi-Pullyu, *The Midnight Folk* is shot through and through with magic. Into it John Masefield poured his love of adventure and the sea and poetry. Superficially *The Midnight Folk* is a story of a treasure-hunt. On other levels it is a picture of night and its wild creatures, and a study of loyalty. Little Kay Harker, with the help of the midnight folk, cat, fox, otter, rat and the rest, and of the Guards, his old discarded toys, defeats the powers of evil and completes the task undertaken by his great-grandfather long ago. In the course of this he flies (by broomstick or bat-wing), swims with otters and mermaids, and sails the Spanish Main in a ship manned by mice. Despite this, the story is never anything less than completely convincing, because Masefield took his own invention perfectly seriously. To him, to Kay and to the reader it matters greatly that the Harker treasure should be restored to its rightful home and that Abner Brown and his men should be defeated. The most improbable of the fantastic events carries conviction because it is described in clear detail. When Kay awoke for the first of his midnight adventures "all things looked more real than usual", and, long before the days of skin-diving, the underwater scenes in the Caribbean are realised in the most beautiful detail. The human and animal characters are drawn without caricature, and this makes Abner an even more sinister villain – "his outside seemed all wooly, white lamb, and the inside all bitey rough wolf" – and a comic character like the cellerman rat no less funny and at the same time quite serious. The unobtrusively lovely prose, the rough music of the verse, the swift action, the nocturnal atmosphere, all contribute to the final effect of *The Midnight Folk*, a great fantasy and a wonderful tale of adventure.

During the 'twenties there were some interesting importations. From the United States came *Tales from Silver Lands* [1925], by the fourth winner of the Newbery Medal, Charles Finger, an Englishman who had gone to sea and had wandered around the world before settling down in Arkansas. He heard the *Tales from Silver Lands* among the Indians of Patagonia and retold them with a high eloquence that somehow avoided artificiality. There were several more of Padraic Colum's noble prose versions of the great stories of the past, notably *The Children of Odin* [1930] with Pogany's illustrations, and a book of myths entitled *Orpheus* which was decorated by an Ukranian artist of startling virtuosity, Boris Artzybasheff. The same artist also collaborated with Ella Young in a book of Celtic tales – *The Wonder Smith and His Son* – which Longmans introduced in 1927.

In 1929 English children met for the first time an American artist (of Bohemian origin) who was to become very dear to them. This was Wanda Gag, whose *Millions of Cats* was the first of a series of picture-books with rhythmic prose and mannered, equally rhythmic black-and-white drawings. The year earlier the oddly named *To and Again* [later reissued as *Freddy's First Adventure*] brought to England the learned and resourceful pig Freddy, an uncompromisingly American creation of Walter R. Brooks. This was followed in 1930 by *More 'To and Again*'. The most original and interesting of the imported books however came from Australia. Norman Lindsay's *The Magic Pudding* [1925] was a kind of national epic of Australia, an uproarious picaresque yarn told with gusto and lack of respect for tradition which comes best from a young nation. The story of Albert the pudding who was both savoury and sweet and who renewed himself after every meal, and of his custodians Barnacle Bill and Sam Sawnoff the penguin, and of the well-mannered Bunyip Bluegum, remains one of the very few comic masterpieces of children's literature.

The success of A. A. Milne encouraged the publication of much verse and, even when the poetry was unlike his, the publisher contrived to give it something of a 'Christopher Robin' look, as in E. V. Lucas's *Playtime and Company* [1925] and Eleanor Farjeon's *Joan's Door* [1926]. Many of the verses in *Joy Street* were reissued in book-form, including those of Roy Meldrum, Rose Fyleman and Hugh Chesterman. Among the new verse of this period was *Real Fairies* [1923] by a writer whose name was to become familiar, Enid Blyton. One adult poem – *Reynard the Fox* – children were to take for their own. Masefield's masterpiece of the English countryside was issued in 1921 with fine illustrations by G. D. Armour, and quickly proved to be one of those rare books to whose appeal there were no limits of age or background. A new poet of standing, Humbert Wolfe, found time to write shapely and witty rhymes for children, notably in *Kensington Gardens* [1927] and *Cursory Rhymes* [1922] for which Albert Rutherston provided equally witty decorations. These were very much of their period, but a handful of the verses deserve revival.

The best of Walter de la Mare's poetry for children had been written by 1920, but several notable collections were published during the 'twenties. In 1922 *Down-a-down-derry* appeared. This was a satisfyingly large book of fairy poems, principally from *Peacock Pie* and *Songs from Childhood*, with delicate illustrations by Dorothy P. Lathrop. *Stuff and Nonsense* [1927] showed him in an unfamiliar mood of frivolity. His collected *Poems for Children* appeared in 1930. Meanwhile, in addition to writing his fine play *Crossings*, which Beaumont published in 1921, he had made the first of the anthologies which were to be in a way the most characteristic of all his contributions to literature. *Come Hither* made its first appearance in 1923, a handsome fat volume with rather heavy woodcuts by Alec Buckels. No previous anthology had revealed so much of the compiler. The introduction "The story of this book' afforded a fascinating glimpse of the boyhood of a poet, and 170 pages of notes "About and Roundabout" gave the editor space in which to gossip about himself, other poets, other books and to quote a generous additional number of poems. In a second edition, in 1924, this section was greatly extended. A recent [1960] new edition has helped to extend the influence of an anthology which achieves, in so decisive a way, two of the functions of such compilations; it displays a clear point of view, and it awakens in the reader a delight in poetry and sends him exploring on his own. A later anthology *Tom Tiddler's Ground* [1932] had a more narrowly educational aim, but this too shed light on both the poetry and the poet.

Compared with the splendid achievements in fantasy, the naturalistic stories of the 'twenties were thin on the ground and not of the first interest. Two enduring characters were born, Ameliaranne in 1920 and Milly-Molly-Mandy in 1928. The first Ameliaranne (*Ameliaranne and the Green Umbrella*) was by Constance Heward, who was to be associated with many in the series, but several other authors contributed stories about this matter-of-fact little girl, so well portrayed in the illustrations of Susan Pearse. All the Milly-Molly-Mandy stories were the work of Joyce L. Brisley. The studies of both characters were distinguished by simplicity and honest, if unsubtle, observation. There was a great deal more subtlety, and as much honesty, in *Marytary*, which appeared in 1928 with pictures by George Morrow. H. B. Creswell wrote this for a real child, and his story has the easy colloquial style which betrays its oral origins. The adventures of Marytary and Johnny Peascod are nearly credible and always set in a recognisable society. Their gentle humour is most endearing.

Writing in the *Times Literary Supplement* in 1959, Rebecca West composed an epitaph for a dead, or at least dying, type of story, the pony book: "These books make it seem likely that from the ponies' point of view pony clubs must have more than their share of club bores, and it is really very difficult to see how these animals could feel any intense emotion for their characterless owners". The pony book came into being in 1929 with one of the best of its kind – *Moorland Mousie* by 'Golden Gorse'. Like most of these stories this was weak in narrative, but was written simply and showed a sound understanding of animal, and some understanding of human, behaviour. Lionel Edward's drawings were of the highest quality of their sort. The best of the animal stories came from abroad. From Norway came *Bambi, a Life in the Woods* which, with John Galsworthy's blessing, appeared under Cape's imprint in 1928. Two Newbery winners came from America,

Will James' *Smoky the Cowhorse* [1926] and Dhan Gopal Mukerji's *Gay-Neck* [1927]. The only English story of comparable quality was Henry Williamson's *Tarka the Otter*, a beautiful and accurate prose poem which the author in no wise intended for children but which they have taken as their own.

There were few adventure stories which had any claim to literary interest. The best were Masefield's period yarn *Jim Davis* [1924] and John Budden's *Jungle John* [1927]. By far the finest of the genre, and one of the best of all time, was the American *The Splendid Journey* [1928], in which Honoré Morrow told the story of an orphan boy on the trail to Oregon. The setting and the historic period were unfamiliar to English readers, but the grandeur, truth and tragedy of this great tale were universal qualities.

One book of the 'twenties defeats classification. In writing *Martin Pippin in the Apple Orchard* [1921] Eleanor Farjeon was thinking not of children but of an English soldier sick for the Sussex downs. When the book first appeared it had none of the physical appearance of a book for children and it was not till 1925 that C. E. Brock's illustrations were added. It is in fact a book, not for children, but for particular people, and those who respond to its gentle melodies may be of any age. It comes near to capturing the mood of adolescent girlhood and it is in this 'age group,' if one must pin down so delicate a butterfly, that it belongs. In its subtle blending of realism and fantasy, of prose and poetry, it is most characteristic of the author whose first major work it was.

Among illustrators of the 'twenties Ernest H. Shepard was the most characteristic of his age. Rackham and Kay Nielson and other 'colour-plate' artists did work of much the kind and quality that had been done for a decade or more. Shepard drew for line-blocks of an economical sort. His methods and his style were of his time, and he matched the humorous homely fantasy of the 'twenties admirably. In addition to the Milne books he did much good work, notably in Grahame's *Dream Days* [1928] and *The Golden Age* [1930], although it was not until 1931 that he reached his best in a new edition of *The Wind in the Willows*.

There was good characteristic work by established artists like F. D. Bedford [*The Magic Fishbone*, 1922], the Brocks, Charles Folkard [*Mother Goose's Nursery Rhymes*, 1924] and even H. R. Millar in a book of which the creator of Worzel Gummidge was co-author [*The Very Good Walkers*, by Marjory Royce and B. E. Todd, 1927]. A distinguished artist in the English water-colour tradition, Rowland Hilder, contributed a *Treasure Island* [1929] to the Oxford Press's new library of children's classics.

(iii) *Information*

In 1919 Arthur Mee founded the *Children's Newspaper*, the third of his major publishing enterprises. (The *Children's Encyclopaedia* had been started in 1908, and *My Magazine* in 1915.) The newspaper looked both backward and forward. The high moral tone and the emphasis on 'improving' knowledge harked back to the informative books of the mid-nineteenth century and earlier. In its concern with contemporary issues and wide-ranging curiosity The *Children's Newspaper* belonged to the post-war world and looked forward to the training in civics which was only slowly and reluctantly being introduced into school curricula.

This was a time of widening horizons. Many more books were published to meet, and to stimulate, an interest in factual knowledge; in particular, publishers saw the advantage of books in series which, when once established, sold themselves on the reputation of earlier titles. Among these were Black's 'Peeps' at history, nature, other countries, etc., (the last including a book on Russia by Edna Waller [1928]), Harrap's 'Romance of Knowledge', and Harry Golding's 'Wonder Books' [*Wonder Book of Wonder*, 1922] which were in advance of their age in the use and lay-out of photographic illustrations.

Although these books were honest attempts to present facts in a simple and interesting way, the 'series' convention offered little scope for individual treatment or imagination. Most of the books were pedestrian, some dull. Literary excellence would have been out of place. For work of creative quality one looked elsewhere, and looked first to America where a writer of Dutch origin was awakening the curiosity and the beginnings of social conscience in young people by entirely original means. Hendrik van Loon's *The Story of Mankind* appeared in an English edition in 1922. His challenging *Liberation of Mankind* appeared in 1926, and *Multiplex Man*, a history of technology, in 1928. Van Loon's bold, accurate simplification, his terse eloquence, and the working drawings with which he brought difficult concepts home sharply and clearly to the reader, marked a long stride forward in the writing and presentation of informative material. Above all Van Loon paid his readers the compliment of expecting them to think for themselves.

It was a long time before factual books of this quality were to be produced in England. On a less imaginative level some good work was done. Among books about animals the most interesting were those of Eric Fitch Daglish [*Animals in Black and White*, 1928, and many others]. Daglish was primarily a wood-engraver, one who combined scientific accuracy with a fine sense of design; he could also write simply and briefly. E. G. Boulenger was a scientist of repute who wrote easily and with humour. His *Aquarium Book* [1925] had illustrations by L. R. Brightwell which emphasised this latter quality. There was a vogue for 'real-life' stories about animals, particularly about improbable pets, like Frances Pitt's *Moses, my Otter* [1927], and *Diana, my Badger* [1929], and Cherry Kearton's *My Friend Toto* [1925] – Toto was a chimpanzee.

Books about history ranged from the conventional (like H. E. Marshall's *Our Island Story* [1920] to the scholarly (the outstanding example of which was *Boys and Girls of History* [1926] by Eileen and Rhoda Power, which, almost for the first time outside historical fiction, brought home to children the 'homeliness' of history). Dorothy M. Stuart's *The Boy Through the Ages*, in the same year, had much the same object, if not quite the same charm. These were for older children; younger readers had Eva Erleigh's *In the Beginning* [1926], with the help of excellent drawings by Mary Adshead, or the two lovely volumes of Eleanor Farjeon's *Mighty Men* [1924–25] which by anecdote and poem appealed unashamedly to the sense of romance and wonder. M. B. Synge [*A Book of Discovery*, 1929] and John Buchan [*Last Secrets*, 1923] looked at the achievements of more recent mighty men, as also, in a less eloquent way, did Arthur Mee in his *Hero Book* [1923]. Many writers were concerned with the adventure of contemporary life: Ellison Hawks' *Book of Remarkable Machinery* [1928] and books by T. C. Bridges and H. H. Tiltman, like *Heroes of Modern Adventure* [1927], among a host of others. Most of these were worthy but uninspired. The first English writer to reflect Van Loon's progressive approach was Amabel Williams-Ellis, whose child's introduction to biology *How You Began* [1928] was followed by a set of biographies *Men Who Found Out* [1929] which looked forward a quarter of a century in its concern with real human problems.

In imaginative writing the 'twenties were dominated by Blackwell's, the publishers of *Joy Street*. The same house issued in 1928 a very charming informative book which, in its simplicity, humour and lack of pretension, is typical of the best of its kind. It is impossible to resist quoting Janet Smalley's title in full: *This is the book that the author made, that tells of the tale of toil and trade, from the orange grove to the marmalade, from the cotton boll to the trimming braid, things that are handled by man and maid, in every house that Jack built.*

CHAPTER 5

RENAISSANCE

IN a number of ways the 'thirties resembled the first years of the twentieth century. Once again the world sat on the edge of the volcano; this time, however, thanks to the mass media of the popular press and the radio, people were more acutely aware of what was happening beyond their immediate surroundings. Technical advances were accompanied, not by increased prosperity but by unemployment and social unrest. Growing materialism was matched by the idealism of the Peace Pledge and the International Brigade. It was an age of contradictions, an age of complacency and of reassessment.

Concern was growing for children and their education, formal and informal. There was evidence of this among librarians. In 1932 the first full examination of library work with children – W. C. Berwick Sayers' *Manual of Children's Libraries* – appeared; and in the previous year the Library Association had undertaken an annual survey of children's books to be entitled *Books to Read*. In 1936 the Carnegie Medal was instituted by the Library Association, in commemoration of Andrew Carnegie's centenary, to honour "a distinguished contribution to children's literature", the first award going not to a representative of the children's book Establishment, but to the most forward-looking of contemporary writers, Arthur Ransome. A year later an Association of Children's Librarians was founded under the inspiration of its first secretary, Eileen H. Colwell, and in the same year a Schools Library Section of the Library Association (later the School Library Association) was established.

Publishers became aware of the growing importance (and potential profit) of the children's market. Dent's saw the value of the library trade and produced a special 'library' edition of their classics in buckram in 1937. A year earlier they had appointed Miss M. C. Carey as their first children's editor, and Grace Allen (later Hogarth) had gone to the Oxford University Press as assistant editor. Mary Treadgold became children's editor of Heinemann's in 1939. A leading writer of 'Rewards', Christine Chaundler, published a 'writer's guide to the juvenile market' entitled *The Children's Author* in 1937.

The criticism of children's books had always been in the hands of (in A. A. Milne's phrase) "some brisk uncle from the Tiny Tots Department". By 1936 there was nothing comparable to the specialist review *Horn Book*, much less Mary Lambarton Becker's children's page in the New York Herald Tribune. Regular responsible reviewing in the national press is still lacking, but in 1936 H. J. B. Woodfield, who had strengthened his natural flair for children's books by experience in teaching, librarianship and bookselling, founded *The Junior Bookshelf* as the first (and still the sole) British journal devoted exclusively to an independent critical examination of children's literature.

Meanwhile, F. J. Harvey Darton's *Children's Books in England* had appeared in 1932. This book, appropriately written by the descendant of a pioneer publisher in this field, explored the origins of children's books, and the social and educational ideas which prompted them, in an exhaustive, authoritative and stimulating fashion.

In the 'thirties books met forces which might be either powerful allies or formidable opponents in cinema and radio. One of the most pervading influences in the production of picture-books for the popular market was Walt Disney. His own creative talent, used fully for the first time in 'Snow White' in 1938, was essentially associated with movement, and designs which on the screen had a quality of lightness and fantasy lost everything but a vulgar facile humour when frozen on the printed page. Disney's characters, seen in innumerable cheap books as well as in toys and ornaments, dominated the imaginations of many children and fixed for ever the visual patterns of an ancient tale. (Only the other day I heard a child whose parents were young when 'Snow White' was first screened name one of the dwarfs as Dopey.) When Wanda Gag made her gentle traditional version of the tale as a corrective to Disney, the English Catalogue listed it not under Gag or Grimm but under Disney!

The influence of radio was almost all for good. B.B.C. programmes awakened an interest in new ideas and subjects, and provided a new platform for writers; they also offered a means of stimulating an interest in books by broadcasting them in dramatised versions or as serial 'dialogue' stories. The organisers of Children's Hour quickly established high standards, literary, social and moral; the contents of *The Children's Hour Annual* which Derek McCulloch edited in 1936 are almost comparable in quality with those of *Joy Street*. Naturally radio found much of its material in the work of established writers, like Mabel Marlowe, Hulme Beaman and Milne; nevertheless Children's Hour began to find writers of its own, like Norman Hunter and Hugh E. Wright whose *Interminable Trudge of Samuel the Snail* (Sammy let his shell as flats for ten ants) was one of the minor pleasures of 1936.

In children's books the 'thirties were a time of experiment. This is not to say that there was any decline in the production of 'Rewards' or other books written to a traditional formula. These continued to appear in large numbers. There were also notable books which belonged to older traditions, particularly in fantasy. Predominantly, however, this was an age of naturalism, the master of which was Arthur Ransome, and which manifested itself vigorously in the books of Eve Garnett and Noel Streatfeild. In the field of picture-books, long the province of comic fantasy, Edward Ardizzone introduced a hero who, however improbable some of his adventures, belonged firmly to the real world.

Numerically the 'thirties were the most productive years of the century; more interesting books and authors made their first appearance even than in the decade of E. Nesbit. It was notably an age of professional writing. Fewer established writers turned to children's books for light relief from their more important labours; writers of the calibre of Noel Streatfeild, who might well have concentrated on writing adult novels, thought it worth while to devote their best energies to writing for children.

(i) *Edward Ardizzone and the picture-book*

The outstanding picture-book artist of the early 'thirties was Clifford Webb, whose *Story of Noah* appeared in 1931, to be followed in 1933 by *Butterwick Farm* and a year later by *A Jungle Picnic*. It was no coincidence that these books were issued by the publishers of Caldecott and Greenaway, for they belonged clearly to the English tradition. Webb was the master of a clean style, with an effectively simplified use of colour and fidelity to his animal models. (The humans were more heavily stylised.) He used the decorative qualities of nature, without falsifying them, rather as Dorothy P. Lathrop was doing in the United States. Her *Animals of the Bible*, which was published in Britain in 1938, makes an interesting comparison with *Noah;* in spite of the very different results, the methods of selection are similar. The weakness of Clifford Webb's books lay in the text; it seemed, almost invariably, as if the pictures had been drawn first and words devised to fit them.

This could never be a criticism of Edward Ardizzone. In his work, word and line seemed to have grown together, and it was impossible to imagine one without the other. Ardizzone was a largely self-taught artist who had already done some illustrating when *Little Tim and the Brave Sea Captain*, in 1936, established him as a maker of picture-books who looked back to the great tradition (he looked to Caldecott rather than Crane and still more to Dicky Doyle and Leech and Rowlandson) but still drew in a style all his own. *Little Tim* was a major landmark in English picture-books, for its fine colour, vigorous action drawing, beautifully simple and vivid prose, and profound understanding of children and their dream fantasies. In this huge book, 13½ inches high and generously produced with gloriously blank pages between each pair of printed ones as a challenge to the emulating talents of young artists, Ardizzone brought fresh air into the nursery. His hero, a real boy, neither prig nor clown, was resourceful and commonplace and pleasingly modest. In 1937 the scene changed to England and the pictures focussed on a heroine, Lucy Brown. *Lucy Brown and Mr. Grimes* (which encountered opposition in the States on grounds of morality!) was a quieter story but showed as firm an understanding of children. In *Tim and Lucy Go to Sea* [1938] hero and heroine came together in a breath-taking adventure.

Two years before *Little Tim* a distinguished visitor had crossed the Channel, Babar the elephant. *The Story of Babar, the Little Elephant* was published by Methuen in 1934 with a benedictary preface by A. A. Milne. This good wine at least needed no such bush; there could have been no doubt about the success of Jean de Brunhoff's creation. This very big book had words and pictures of the utmost simplicity, but it was the simplicity of great art. The wide double-spread pictures were full of movement and fascinating detail; children could pore over each for a long time. The sincerity and serious humour of the story was equally appealing. An immortal character can hardly have been established with fewer words or lines. Five more enchanting stories followed, some of them published posthumously for Jean de Brunhoff had died in 1937. They seemed not so much sequels as single facets of one great original.

From France too came the 'Pere Castor' books of Lida, with Rojan [Rojankovsky]'s exquisite decorations. *Mischief the Squirrel* and *Quipic the Hedgehog* [both 1938] contrasted strikingly with *Babar*. These were highly sophisticated works of art in which the relationship between picture and text was worked out most carefully. Benjamin Rabier's was a homelier talent; his *Old Fox in the Wood* [1936] and *Thirty Fables* [1938] had a sweetness of humour which made an immediate appeal.

Kathleen Hale added a portrait to the gallery of memorable characters in 1938 when *Orlando the Marmalade Cat* appeared. Technically hers were among the most accomplished drawings of the century and almost the best in lithography. She rendered the texture of her hero's fine fur-coat, and that of his wife Grace, with incredible fidelity. Kathleen Hale's stories were thin, and clumsily constructed, and she crammed her pictures rather uncomfortably with, it must be admitted, highly relevant detail. Her cat-world, for although humans and other animals inhabit it cats are the dominant race, was consistent throughout, and her humour, not always in impeccable taste, pervaded every corner of her books.

If Kathleen Hale had a fault, it was a reluctance to leave anything out. Joan Kiddell-Monroe was a master of selection; one feels that her ideal is, like the Bellman's map, a "perfect and absolute blank"! Like Ardizzone she found her personal style immediately, and all her characteristics were to be seen in her first book, *In His Little Black Waistcoat* [1939]. There was not more story than was needed to provide the artist with an opportunity to draw animals, but each huge page (the book was 15 inches high) was designed with the utmost discretion, with a subtle balancing of black and white masses.

Stephen Bone and his wife Mary Adshead broke new ground in their *Little Boy and His House* [1936], an attempt, beautifully successful, to convey information in terms of the picture-book. The little boy sought advice about how to build himself a house, and received conflicting opinions from people of different races. In the end he realised that "it all depends on where you live and what you have to build with". This unexceptionable lesson was conveyed with a minimum of words and with bold, richly colourful drawings.

The Story of Horace has the noble inevitability of classical tragedy; it seems like a folk-tale. Alice Coats always thought it was of American origin. In 1937 her picture-book version, drawn originally for her private amusement, was published by Faber. Few children's stories had been so ruthless – or so funny. Horace, the bear who ate his way through an entire family, has won a place among the unforgettable characters of children's literature. *Phewtus the Squirrel* has been almost forgotten, but his appearance in 1939 deserves mention, for this was the first book of V. H. Drummond and contained much of the quality which distinguished her more successful post-war work. It had a quiet humour, a feeling for odd and characteristic phrases, and an appreciation for London's parkland, as sincere – if less memorably expressed – as those of *Miss Anna Truly*.

In the 'thirties the first important invasion from America began. The American picture-book reached heights not exceeded since in the early 'thirties. The impetus came largely from New Americans who had immigrated from Europe after the war and who brought to a new country the traditions and imagery of many countries. In 1937 the American Library Association instituted the Caldecott Medal to recognise quality in the making of picture-books, and there was no shortage of candidates. Some of the best of the American picture-books were published in English editions; others were imported by Combridge's of Birmingham and sold mainly to public libraries. To those children, and to publishers and artists, who met them, their vigour and colour were a tremendous stimulus. Among the most interesting and influential were the Petershams, with their reverent *Christ Child* [1933] and other Bible books and their equally interesting story books [*The Story Book of Clothes*, 1936] and, free of the inhibitions of Biblical or instructional subject-matter, the enchanting *Get-a-way and Hary Janos* [1935]. Willy Pogany had been known in England for many years, but nothing he had done in the 'twenties surpassed the blazing colours of *The Golden Cockerel* [1939]. Boris Artzybasheff also brought the gorgeous colours and patterns of the East to his *Seven Simeons* [1937] which was distinguished also by mastery of a most intricate and artificial technique. Kate Seredy's *The White Stag* [1937], nobly written and illustrated, used a narrower range of resources with superb assurance.

Not all American picture-books were on this exalted level. Lois Lenski's skilful homeliness was exactly right for her gentle stories *The Little Sailing Boat* [1938] and *The Baby Car* [1937], and Munro Leaf was a master of simplicity and humour, whether accompanied by his own match-stick drawings [*Manners Can be Fun*, 1937, or *Robert Francis Weatherbee*, 1936], or by the rich sophistication of Robert Lawson in *The Story of Ferdinand* [1937] or *Wee Gillis* [1938]. Robert Lawson was the illustrator also of Richard Atwater's delightful *Mr. Popper's Penguins* [1938]. Marjorie Flack, in many stories about the dog Angus [*Angus and the Ducks*, 1933, and others] and still more in *The Story about Ping* [1935], in which she was supported by Kurt Wiese's masterly drawings, achieved the simplicity which comes only from art. Kurt Wiese also illustrated a fine folk-tale (or pseudo-folk-tale) by Claire Huchet Bishop, *The Five Chinese Brothers* [1939]. From the States, too, came Clare T. Newberry's cat books, *Mittens* [1937] and others, beautifully printed in photogravure, which surpassed Kathleen Hale's in fidelity but not in humour. The best of Ludwig Bemelmans was seen here only in imported copies, but his *Hansi* had an English edition in 1935, and his richly comical drawings for Munro Leaf's *Noodle* (Noodle was a dachshund who needed a double-spread for his full deployment) appeared in 1938. In 1939 a book of startling originality was published by Country Life. *And to Think that I Saw it on Mulberry Street* was the first book of 'Dr. Seuss' [Theodor Seuss Geisel], an artist of great power, great eccentricity and greater humour. No later book of his exceeded the fantastic and charming dream-fantasies of his first.

(ii) *Fantasy and fairy tale*

In 1835 Hans Christian Andersen wrote in a letter: "I have started on one or two tales, told for children, and I fancy I have been successful". To celebrate this centenary the Cambridge University Press published in 1935 a new version by R. P. Keigwin of the first four tales in a most attractive little book with wood engravings, which could hardly have been closer to the spirit of the stories, by Gwen Raverat. Keigwin's translation was particularly happy in its rendering of the colloquial tales "The Tinder Box" and "Little Claus and Big Claus". A larger edition issued on the same occasion by Cobden-Sanderson used an older and more 'literary' translation, but this book was notable for the wonderfully poetical illustrations of Rex Whistler. In this company a third centenary volume, from Hutchinson, seemed trivial, in spite of the elegance of Joyce Mercer's decorations. Two other translations of Andersen, by H. L. Braekstad and Paul Leyssac, followed in 1937 without disturbing the pre-eminence of M. R. James and Keigwin.

Andersen's greatness had been the result of an unique fusing of poetry, homeliness, humour and memory. It is for these qualities that one searches, usually in vain, among the invented fairy-stories of these years. Homeliness and memory were characteristics of Alison Uttley. A book for adults [*The Country Child*] in 1931 gave hopes that here was potentially an individual writer for children. A book which recorded so accurately and perceptively the everyday deeds and sensations of childhood contained the raw material of children's literature. Some of this country lore spilled over into *Moonshine and Magic* [1932] and into *Candlelight Tales* [1936], which explored the drama and magic latent in nursery rhymes; but Alison Uttley found her happiest vein in *Tales of the Four Pigs*, the first of the sweetly humorous tales of Sam Pig, in 1939. Even closer to Andersen were the stories in *The Spider's Palace* [1931]. Richard Hughes understood the fantastic logic of a child's mind, and applied it rigidly to a series of delightfully ridiculous situations in these tales. Hughes' deceptively simple prose concealed a rich imagination and a deeply understanding mind. Some of the same qualities were evident in Mairin Cregan's Irish *Old John* [1937] and M. Melville Balfour's Cornish legends *The Vanishing Mayor of Padstow* [1938].

This was a notable period for short stories written with style and humour. J. B. Morton, who as 'Beachcomber' was the most mordant of humorous journalists, wrote some neat mock-fairy tales in *The Death of the Dragon* [1934]; these were children's stories for adults. No adult values crept into Catherine Scales' *Gay Company* [1938] and her still more successful *Nugger Nonsense* [1939]; her dachshund hero had a charmingly tough character. Something of the same quality appeared in *The White Duck* by Ann Scott-Moncrieff [1935]. These beautifully written tales, for which Rojan provided lively drawings, lacked originality in invention, but a fine Scots strain made them strongly individual. Olwen Bowen's were more conventional stories, but the naïve humour of her Hepzibah stories [*The Hepzibah Omnibus*, 1936] made a direct appeal to children; so did the rustic Canadian comedy of Thornton W. Burgess's tales like *Little Joe Otter* [1935].

Some memorable comic characters were invented during the 'thirties: Mary Plain, the charming bear of Berne, [*All Mary*, 1931], Mumfie the elephant [1935], and Claudius the bee [1936]. These were all topical creations, whose stories have a certain period flavour. Worzel Gummidge was timeless; in the Scarecrow of Scatterbrook, who was born in 1936, Barbara Euphan Todd made a character to stand beside Pooh in the gallery of the immortals. This moody disagreeable boggart has developed a life independent of the books in which he has appeared. The books themselves, it must be admitted, have no great distinction in writing or invention. Mary Poppins is a much more subtle creation, although she has never won the universal acclaim of Worzel Gummidge. In four exquisite books (*Mary Poppins*, [1934] was the first), P. L. Travers developed a most original and consistent heroine. Mary Poppins is a nursemaid, terribly convincing in her severity and high standards, putting down her wards with ruthless efficiency, perfect but for her yard-wide vein of conceit; she is also, and this is one of the most delicious surprises in children's literature, magical. Two other notable characters survive only in Puffin editions. In happy partnership with Heath Robinson, Norman Hunter created the absent-minded inventor, Professor Branestawm, whose "incredible adventures", published in 1933, had a big success on the

B.B.C. Children's Hour. Professor Branestawm was an enjoyable caricature, but Mr. Leakey was a character. *My Friend, Mr. Leakey* [1937] was the only book for children of the distinguished scientist, J. B. S. Haldane. In it he produced marvellous alchemy by combining science and magic. There is a strange realism in the description of Mr. Leakey's dinner, served by an octopus and cooked on its own red-hot body by a small dragon. The marvels of Mr. Leakey are not less wonderful for being described with circumstantial detail.

The principal event in poetry was the publication of *The Poet's Tongue* in 1935. This was the most interesting anthology since *Come Hither*. W. H. Auden and John Garrett had cut through the barrier of pretension and humbug which kept many children from an enjoyment of poetry. *The Poet's Tongue* showed that the most artless of nursery rhymes and popular songs had a share of the creative vitality of true poetry.

There were no new discoveries among poets. Euphan [B. E. Todd]'s verses in the 'Punch' manner – *The Seventh Daughter* – were neat rather than original. By far the best work was done by two veterans, Walter de la Mare and Eleanor Farjeon. De la Mare wrote little that was new for children in the 'thirties, apart from the *Stories from the Bible* [1931] and his anthology of *Animal Stories* [1939]; his energies were dedicated to other work, including the characteristic study of childhood, so rich a source-book for all who study the creative impulse in children, *Early One Morning in the Spring* [1935]. His one book of original verse for children was of the greatest interest. This was *This Year, Next Year* [1937], a set of verses prompted, much as those in *Flora* had been, by drawings by a young artist, Harold Jones. As a picture-book *This Year, Next Year* resembled those of Kate Greenaway; it remains one of the finest examples of the blending of word and line. Unfortunately the book (including the originals) was destroyed in the Blitz, and it has never been reprinted.

The 'thirties saw Eleanor Farjeon at her best in verse and prose. She always worked best for an occasion, in sets of related verses like those in *Over the Garden Wall* [1933] and *Sing for Your Supper* [1938] or in sets of verse and prose like *Martin Pippin in the Daisy Field* [1937]. Her facile but seldom trivial rhymes, the melodies and rhythms which played continuously in her head, the mellow wisdom and kindliness of her thought, gave to her writing at this time a very personal character and distinction.

The 'thirties were perhaps the richest of all decades in fantasy. Some

of those now almost forgotten – Stella Gibbons' *The Untidy Gnome* [1935] and A. E. Coppard's *Pink Furniture* [1930] ("a tale for lovely children with noble natures") deserved a better fate. John Buchan's *The Magic Walking-stick* [1932], Richard Hatch's *The Curious Lobster* [1937], and G. Dewi Robert's *The House that was Forgotten* [1935] explored fascinating aspects of magic; so did J. W. Dunne's *An Experiment with St. George* [1939] in which, with the help of Rojankovsky's wonderful drawings, he tried out in a children's story the theories of time which he had made his own.

For all their incidental and fundamental humour, the major fantasies of this period were profoundly serious; these jokes were not to be laughed at! Ursula Moray Williams' *Adventures of the Little Wooden Horse* [1938] is a story of heroism and endurance; it is the kind of long story that Andersen might have written. The hero is hero *malgre lui*: "I'm a quiet little horse . . . and the thought of going out into the wide world breaks my heart", but the reader feels most deeply the sufferings he endures during his long journeyings.

One also takes seriously the high adventure of *The Box of Delights* [1935], so much so that one reaches the conventional ending (the hero woke up and discovered that it had all been a dream) with a shock of disappointment and loss. There had been no such cheating in *The Midnight Folk*, which had been reissued with Rowland Hilder's fine decorations in 1931. In *The Box of Delights* the hero of both stories, Kay Harker, was several years older, and Masefield showed with great understanding the last fine flowering of a child's imagination before the prison-house closes around him.

A characteristic of *The Box of Delights* was the blend of timeless and contemporary in the magic. The agent of good might be the Bishop of Tadchester or Herne the Hunter; danger came from pirates or fake curates; travel was by magic box or car or aeroplane. There was something of the same skilful blending of incongruities in Patricia Lynch's *The Turf-cutter's Donkey* [1934]. Patricia Lynch had grown up in the magic climate of Ireland and had learnt her story-telling from one of the Irish masters of this art. The Irish had always been distinguished more for gusto and eloquence than for discipline, and in this and later books Patricia Lynch sometimes let her narrative wander dangerously. Her sense of wonder, in everyday things as much as in magic, gives to her writing its individual quality. She reached the height of her powers in *The King of the Tinkers* [1938] and *The Grey Goose of Kilnevin* [1939]. The latter book fused the marvellous and the homely into a story of very great beauty. Sheila, who was sent by Fat Maggie to buy three pounds of butter from Bridgie Swallow and on this harmless errand meets adventures in and out of this world, is the best of a long series of sweet, practical peasant heroines; and Betsy, the goose who shares her adventures, provides the touchstone of reality in a story of marvels.

Both Kay Harker and Sheila bridged easily the gap between present and past, and the same theme dominated Hilda Lewis's notable fantasy *The Ship that Flew* [1939]. Peter bought the ship that flew for all the money he had in the world – and a bit over. It was the ship that Odin had given to Frey as his wedding gift, and with it Peter and his brothers and sisters travelled in time and space. Of all the many stories prompted by E. Nesbit, this is the closest in spirit to the original (although there is little humour), and like Nesbit's it becomes more serious as the theme is developed. The greatest problem the writer of fantasy has to solve is how to get rid of the magic and so bring the story to an end; Hilda Lewis's solution is conspicuously satisfactory.

The Sword in the Stone was not written for children; indeed so spontaneous an outpouring of fun and beauty and wisdom could only have been written to please the author. It was nevertheless a book for children to take for their own. T. H. White is an Anglo-Irish sportsman, naturalist and mediaevalist. In *The Sword in the Stone* he brought his expert knowledge, together with an acute realistic sense of humour, to the story of the boyhood of King Arthur. It is a very funny book; the broad farce of the scene in which King Pellinore and Sir Grummore joust, the fantasy of Merlin's domestic economy (his dishes wash themselves up), the good humour of the festive scenes, bring a variety of reactions from loud laughter to inward delight. It is also intensely serious, for White was concerned to show the basis for education in kingship. The Wart (the future king) learnt his art from the animal, vegetable and mineral worlds, and the climax, in which he summoned up all his strength, skill and wisdom to take the sword from the stone, was a scene of the utmost splendour. With fine timing, the author brought back the comedy in the last pages. This was an entirely original book in its conception; in tone, invention and writing it is fully worthy of its great idea.

While *The Sword in the Stone* was a book for adults which some children have adopted, *The Hobbit* was written for children (the author devised it originally for the amusement of his own family) and taken over by adults. This was partly because J. R. R. Tolkien, having undertaken his story lightly, seems to have been taken by surprise by it and to have found successive layers of meaning in it. This is not uncommon – there are depths in *Alice* and *The Wind in the Willows* – but only Tolkien has made his children's book the starting point of a great fantastic and romantic allegory [*The Lord of the Rings*, 1954–55]. *The Hobbit, or, There and Back Again* appeared in 1927. It was the work of a Professor of Anglo-Saxon at Oxford. Tolkien had made the early literature and still earlier traditions of England (and the countries from which the English came) particularly his own, and it was his scholarship that helped to give authority to his story about the hobbit's quest, for he could define with great precision the differences between dwarves, elves, goblins and trolls and describe the society in which each lived. *The Hobbit* carries great conviction; it reads more like history than romance. It also blends the heroic and the homely with extraordinary skill. Bilbo Baggins, the Hobbit, who liked comfort and staying at home but who became a great traveller and nearly a hero, is a most subtle character. So too is the dragon Smaug who stood guard over the treasure of the dwarves. *The Hobbit* is an exciting story of adventure, a tragedy with comic episodes, a picaresque romance with strands of magic in it, an historical novel about the remote past which, by the author's craft, becomes more real than the present. It is better to use superlatives sparingly, but this, by any standards, is a great book.

Each new generation has to meet the traditional tales of the past and for each new interpreters are needed. Children in the 'thirties were fortunate in having, from America, a new and inspired guide to the fairy tales of the Brothers Grimm. Wanda Gag had heard these tales as a child from an old grandmother who knew them not as words in a book but as living tales told aloud by the fireside. Remembering this Wanda Gag translated the stories anew and illustrated them in a manner totally free of urban sophistication. *Tales from Grimm* [1937] was a splendid reminder of the fine story-telling and the pervading humour of these much ill-used tales.

No other contemporary collections of folk-tales were of this quality, but Harcourt Williams, a distinguished actor who had made an art of story-telling, kept the oral quality predominant in his *Tales from Ebony* [1934], and Amabel Williams-Ellis, in *Fairies and Enchanters* [1933], made unpretentious versions of English tales. Angela Thirkell's German stories *The Grateful Sparrow* [1935] were more consciously artful. From America came two fine collections by Post Wheeler – *Russian Wonder Tales* [1931] and *Albanian Wonder Tales* [1936], and an admirable version of the classical Indian *Ramayana* [*Rama: the Hero of India*, 1931] by Dhan Gopal Mukerji. Two most interesting collections, one a work of scholarship, extended the repertory of the story-teller; in *Salam the Mouse-Deer* [1938] A. Hillman and W. W. Skeat introduced the rich folk-lore of Malaya; and Geraldine Elliot's *The Long Grass Whispers* [1939] showed many of the same themes occuring among the N'Gomi of Central Africa.

As well as folk-tales the stories of Homer offer a challenge to each generation, and in 1937 G. B. Harrison, the Shakespearian scholar, wrote his version of the Odyssey in *The Wanderings of Ulysses* following it three years later with *New Tales of Troy*. Harrison's simple dignified prose was equally evident in *New Tales from Shakespeare* [1938] and *New Tales from Malory* [1939].

(iii) *Into the past*

Although there was no shortage of stories of the Empire-building school, the 'thirties were also a time of historical questioning, and several writers showed themselves willing to present an unconventional picture of the past. The first important book of this kind was Naomi

Mitchison's *The Hostages* [1930]. Naomi Mitchison, a member of a distinguished family (J. S. Haldane was her father, Viscount Haldane her uncle and J. B. S. Haldane her brother) and a person of aggressive individuality, chose in these stories not to write about famous events and people – even the Battle of Hastings is told at second hand – but to show the slow changes of history and the lives of ordinary people. She linked her nine stories with a wise and thought-provoking commentary which gave point to the short dramatic stories.

In his first historical work for children, *King Richard's Land* [1933], L. A. G. Strong took the familiar theme of the Peasant's Revolt and told it with considerable liveliness but fairly conventionally and with no great evocation of atmosphere. *Mr. Sheridan's Umbrella* [1935] was unusual in subject and most successful in performance. His picture of Prinny's Brighton was delightfully done and he lavished on Sheridan the craft of the professional novelist. Most interesting was the use, for dramatic effect, of the technology of the umbrella factory. In *The Fifth of November* [1937] Strong gave new life to the well-worn story of the Gunpowder Plot, first by his sympathetic treatment of the conspirators, and then by his device of indirect narrative. The story is told in the present; children become interested in Guy Fawkes and study the period so effectively that one of them lives himself into the past and shares the sensations of the conspirators. The method is not quite successful, but it does give to the story an added sense of actuality. The historical background, effectively portrayed in Jack Matthew's fine illustrations, was particularly well done.

A similar 'time' device was used, far more successfully, by Alison Uttley in *A Traveller in Time* [1939]. In this, by far the author's finest book, Alison Uttley went back to the memories and dreams of her own childhood in a Derbyshire farmhouse. She created a young heroine who was able to go through the door into the past and to share in the fortunes of the Babington family in the time of Queen Elizabeth. No book kept a more sensitive balance between past and present, and the author used the device of 'time' to bring home the timelessness of life in a remote country house. Penelope found herself quickly at home in either century, and so, in her company, does the reader. The book was written with great simplicity, and this gave increased effectiveness to the brooding melancholy which informed it. A sad, beautiful book, it contained everything that Alison Uttley had to offer of country lore, human understanding and feeling for past and present.

In the year of *A Traveller in Time*, Elfrida Vipont (under the pseudonym of 'Charles Vipont') showed an unconventional view of history in *Blow the Man Down*, a strong story of action into which was inextricably woven a theme of religious conscience. Geoffrey Trease's early historical novels were, in their different way, equally surprising. In his first story for children, *Bows Against the Barons* [1934], published by a leading 'Left Wing' publisher, he showed Robin Hood as the protector of the people against their enemies of the Establishment. The story was rather naïvely partisan, but it at least had a point of view. In later books, like *In the Land of the Mogul* [1938], which dealt with the East India Company, and *Cue for Treason* [1940], which started like a tract against enclosures and became an Elizabethan spy story, the point of view was not less pronounced, but it was not allowed to ride the author at the expense of the story.

Not all historical stories were as strongly individualistic as these, but the more conventional tales were not necessarily less soundly historical. Wallace B. Nichols' *King Perkin's Knight* [1938] about Perkin Warbeck's rebellion, Florence Bone's *Lads of Lud* [1936] which showed the Luddite riots from a standpoint which could not have pleased Geoffrey Trease, and the same author's *A Coach for Fanny Burney* [1938], Harriette Campbell's *A Royal Princess* [1934], which skilfully adapted Margaret Irwin's *Royal Flush* for young readers, Marjorie Bowen's professional *Trumpet and the Swan* [1938] with an excellent portrait of Stuart London, and several highly competent books by Carola Oman, notably *Ferry the Fearless* [1936] and *Alfred, King of the English* [1939], were all equally scholarly and entertaining. There was nothing revolutionary in the history of Harriet Powell's *The World was Gay* [1936], but the book deserves particular comment for the author's unusual choice of a Victorian setting. From America, Elizabeth Janet Gray recaptured in most masterly fashion the atmosphere of Georgian Edinburgh in *Young Walter Scott* [1938]. Perhaps the most distinguished historical story was *Columbus Sails* [1939]. A most talented young illustrator, C. Walter Hodges, matched his powerful and dramatic pictures with prose of a rare simplicity and dignity. Physically, this was one of the few British books which challenged comparison with the best contemporary American work; in mastery of words and pictures its only peer was from America, Kate Seredy's *The White Stag* [1938], a story of Attila the Hun which the Hungarian-born artist told with passionate eloquence and for which she drew lithographs of extraordinary range and power. To compare her's and Hodges' books is to see the difference between involvement and splendid detachment.

(iv) *Arthur Ransome and the story of adventure*

There had been, as has been seen, previous families of self-reliant children occupying themselves with worthwhile practical tasks, but these had been isolated phenomena. A book like *The Slowcoach* had not established a school of open-air stories; *Bevis* had devotees rather than followers. *Two Little Savages* encouraged boys to do things for themselves, but it had few imitators. It was left to Arthur Ransome to change the course of literature. Not since E. Nesbit had a single writer exercised so powerful an influence.

Ransome was no theorist. He simply wrote of what interested him. He had always loved the Lakes and sailing and fishing; he enjoyed living rough and looking after himself. When he found that some young friends of his – mostly girls – wanted a story, he adapted one about Windermere and its small boats and about camping and adventures in which the dangers were very nearly real. He put into the book the children he knew, changing sexes where necessary to get an interesting balance, and he drew himself into the picture as the irascible, kindly Captain Flint. The result was *Swallows and Amazons*, which appeared in 1930 in a business-like plain edition, without illustrations but with rather ornate end-paper maps by Steven Spurrier. In the next nine years seven sequels were published, beginning with *Swallowdale* with Clifford Webb's illustrations – and the same artist also illustrated the second edition of *Swallows and Amazons* – in 1931.

One of the qualities which distinguished Arthur Ransome's work from that of almost every other writer for children was that his characters developed in succeeding books. The author also grew with every book. *Swallows and Amazons* was a story of great charm and freshness. Few books have started better; the picture of Roger tacking across the field on his laborious homeward voyage is delightful and authentic. The children however were playing at adventure; they made their own hazards. When John, in *Swallowdale*, sank 'Swallow', reality stepped in. John stopped playing and found himself facing responsibility and rising to it. In *Winter Holiday* [1933] the transition from invented to real adventure was further advanced, and the process was completed in 1937 with *We didn't mean to go to sea*. In this magnificent story, the most concentrated which Ransome wrote, there was no invention at all; 'Goblin', moored in Harwich Roads, slipped her anchor, and John, faced with decisions of adult proportions, sailed her across to Holland. Ransome tested the story himself in the North Sea, and gave it unmistakable authenticity. In a very different way *Coot Club*

[1934] dealt with real problems, practical and moral, and, with a change of scene to the Norfolk Broads, introduced some new and delectable characters. The Carnegie Medal-winning *Pigeon Post* [1936] was not the best of the early stories, but it was characteristic of Ransome's work. The Swallows, Amazons, and Ds, playing so very earnestly at mining, climbing and camping, were admirable in their dedication and industry; only adults would laugh at their seriousness. The book was particularly notable for the development of the character of Dick, who had appeared first in *Winter Holiday*. A lesser writer would have made fun of Dick, who is spectacled, clever and a bit of a swot. Ransome showed how such a boy could at times become a key figure in the group; intelligence and knowledge were not to be despised. Titty, who had been rather tiresomely 'keen' in the first stories, came into her own, too, in *Pigeon Post*. The long passage in which she conquered her own repulsion and divined water for the camp is in Ransome's finest vein of accurate reporting; it is also most profound observation of behaviour.

Peter Duck [1932] stands apart from the other stories. Although it was written with all Ransome's care over practical detail, it had no pretence to probability. It was rather the kind of tall yarn that Captain Flint would have told the children when in expansive mood.

After the first two books, Ransome provided his own illustrations. These were superficially peculiar, for he had little technique in draughtsmanship. The queer drawings had one overwhelming advantage over other artist's work; they illustrated just those points on which elucidation was needed. The pictures were in fact working drawings which showed how the numerous technical problems in the stories were worked out.

Ransome's qualities were literary, practical and social. He wrote supremely well – in a leisurely fashion except in crises – in precise, simple words. He indulged in no tricks and avoided cheap appeals to emotion. When he touched the heart, as at the end of *We didn't mean to go to sea*, the effect was the more powerful. He killed laziness in the writing of children's stories by facing honestly the practical problems which each story presented. Where an earlier writer would have been content to say what happened, Ransome always described *how* it happened. He also (and not artificially as in the old moral tales but because he had developed his own strong standards of moral and social conduct) introduced morality into his stories. His characters were all aware of the need to accept responsibility and to behave as members of a community. He never preached, indeed never thought of preaching, but his own beliefs made the firm foundation of everything he wrote. In the most unobtrusive way his are *good* books.

Every writer of stories of adventure in the open-air since 1930 has owed a debt to Ransome. Nowhere was the debt more apparent, or more sincerely acknowledged, than in *The Far-Distant Oxus* [1937]. This was written by two schoolgirls, Katherine Hull and Pamela Whitlock, who had enjoyed the 'Swallows and Amazons' stories so much that they were compelled to write something of the same kind. There were obvious signs of immaturity in *The Far-Distant Oxus;* it nevertheless showed considerable inventive powers and real subtlety in characterisation. Ransome contributed a characteristically generous introduction. There were two sequels in the same vein, but, as the writers grew up, with some loss of spontaneity.

Garry Hogg's 'Explorer' stories had spirit and accuracy. The author tested them himself by walking and cycling over the ground, and they have a feeling for the countryside and an intelligent concern with cultural as well as social and practical matters. Their weakness was in the portrayal of character. *Explorers awheel* [1938] was followed in the next year by *Explorers on the Wall*.

Initially, at least, M. E. Atkinson's stories were more interesting. *August Adventure*, published in 1936, was a lively, inventive story about well-contrasted and individual children. As the stories proceeded, however, (they came out one a year) the Lockitt's endless search for adventure became tedious. Ransome's children, after the first book, did not have to look for adventure; it evolved naturally from circumstances and personality.

Although these family sagas had some quality, and others, even better, were to be started in a few years' time, the best of the open-air stories in the Ransome tradition were individual books. Conor O'Brien would no doubt have written *Two Boys Go Sailing* [1936] if Ransome had never lived, for he was writing of things he knew and loved, but Ransome had prepared an audience for this fine, authentic tale of adventure. Elizabeth Yates' *High Holiday* [1938] also rang true. The hazards of mountaineering in Switzerland were sufficient material for an accurate, well-observed story. In *Furlong Farm* [1938] Eleanor Helme, a prolific and consistent writer of no great individuality, found an admirable subject in the activities of a Young Farmers' Club.

Ransome's books coincided with a revival of interest in Richard Jefferies. Both reflected a reaction against the increasing urbanisation of English life. The Jefferies revival was largely the result of Henry

Williamson's passionate advocacy; Richard Jefferies was an unseen character in every one of Williamson's books, and through him for the first time a full critical appraisal of this complex genius became possible. A new edition of *Bevis* in 1932 had the support of Ernest H. Shepard's illustrations – some of the best he ever did – and a new generation was admitted to the wonderful country, with its realistic adventures and its mystical experiences, which lies around the New Sea.

Ransome's children were not pony-mad but in the climate created by his stories the pony-book flourished. The somewhat cramping conventions of this genre had not yet become fixed, and some individual and attractive work was done, notably by Joanna Cannan, Moyra Charlton and Primrose Cumming. Joanna Cannan's *A Pony for Jean* [1936] has been a model for almost every succeeding writer; it was based on sound knowledge of riding but was not, as most pony-books have been, cluttered with technical detail to the exclusion of any human interest. It was excellently illustrated by Anne Bullen. Good illustrations, by Lionel Edwards, also distinguished Moyra Charlton's *Tally-Ho* [1932], but she had a better story in *The Midnight Steeplechase* of the same year. Primrose Cumming set her stories pleasantly in the countryside, whether of the Border country in *Doney* [1934] or of Kent in *Rachel of Romney* [1939]. In *Ben* [1939] she turned to a working horse in a brief restrained text to accompany an impressive sequence of photographs by Harold Burdekin. There was an unusually high standard of illustration in most pony-books of the time, many of them based on pencil drawings; the artists included Lionel Edwards, D. L. Mays (in a book by Allen Chaffee, *Wandy the Wild Pony* [1933]), Anne Bullen, and others. Only one book (if one excepts that extraordinary 'tall story', half fairy tale, half psychological study, *National Velvet* [1935] which is hardly about a 'pony' and is scarcely for children) had the quality which demands recognition in its own right, not as an example of a genre; this was *Hobby Horse Hill* [1939] in which Lavinia Davis captured some of the mystery as well as the clean air of Dartmoor.

Country Life were leading publishers of books in this category. Not all were strictly, or even particularly 'pony' books. *On'y Tony* [1935] was as much concerned with the rider as the pony, and the same author (Brenda E. Spender) showed keen and humorous observation in her *Mock Uncle* [1932] with brilliant illustrations by J. H. Dowd. Another of this kind was *David's New World* [1937] which introduced a new team of author-illustrators who were to do distinguished work, Vernon Stokes and Cynthia Harnett.

Although the Swallows and Amazons did not go much for organised games, 'sports' stories were a by-product of Ransome's success. Dent's introduced a series of these, including an expert introduction to golf, *Family Golf* [1938] by Eleanor E. Helme, herself a class player, and a richly humorous cricketing story *The Saturday Match* [1937] by Hugh de Selincourt.

This was one of the richest periods for authentic stories about animals, another manifestation of the longing to escape from urban civilization which contributed to the phenomenal success of 'Grey Owl'. This picturesque pseudo-Indian was a personality rather than a writer, but *The Men of the Last Frontier* [1931], *Pilgrims of the Wild* [1935], and a less interesting book designed especially for children *Sajo and her Beaver People* [1935] had many young readers. Henry Williamson's nature stories enjoyed a great success, following a new edition of *Tarka the Otter* with fine wood-engravings by C. F. Tunnicliffe. Another writer with something of the same exquisite observation was Ernest Lewis whose story of a sheepdog *Beth* appeared in 1934. These were animal books adopted by children but not written for them. R. L. Haig-Brown's stories were for children and adults equally. *Silver* [1931] a story of a salmon, and *Pool and Rapid*, a portrait of a river, lacked a little of Williamson's microscopically exact style; they were for that reason rather more easily read.

The 'Junior Country Life' Library had some good animal-stories, notably those of M. E. Buckingham about India. *Argh* [1935] was a competent story about a tiger. C. M. Enriques also wrote about India in *Khyberie* [1934], but this had a strong human interest. There was a more authentic Indian note in *Leap-Home and Gentlebrawn* [1932], a most beautifully written story of two monkeys. Some of the best of these books were importations, two with Australian settings: Frank D. Davison's *Man-Shy* [1934], later published as *Red Heifer*, and Charles J. Finger's story of a sheep-dog, *A Dog at His Heels* [1937]. There were several distinguished stories by a Danish writer, Svend Fleuron, notably *The Wild Horses of Iceland* [1933], and a rarely beautiful story from Russia about a lynx, *Mourzouk*, by Vitaly Bianchi [1937]. Here perhaps belongs the first of Chiang Yee's stories for children, *Chin-Pao and the Giant Panda* [1939], but his is a delicate art which defies classification.

(v) *Followers of Emil*

The first English edition of *Emil and the Detectives* in 1931 was a major landmark. This 'tale of adventure and romance', as Walter de la Mare called it, was something new in adventure stories, even if it was also, by the same authority, like the folk-tale of "the youngest of the three brothers who goes out to seek his fortune . . . and gets it". It was a story of real children in a contemporary city setting. It showed all the life of the city, but all from the viewpoint of a small boy. It was unusual in having a 'model boy' for a hero, and also in adopting a conversational and informal style.

The effect of *Emil* was immediate and has been lasting, particularly on the Continent where it is clearly to be seen in recent books by Paul Berna and others. The book was very popular in England, running through several editions, and being published here in French and German and in dramatic forms; there was also a less successful sequel *Emil and the Three Twins* [1935]. There was much of *Emil* in two excellent books introduced into England from the Continent, *Henry against the Gang* [1936] in which J. H. Johansen's debt to Erich Kastner was clearly apparent, and H. J. Kaeser's *Mimff* [1939], an excellent book in its own right and a most memorable portrait of a boy. Among native English books the effect of *Emil* is most apparent in 'detective' stories by T. F. W. Hickey, *The Unexpected Adventure* [1935] and *Bulldog Sheila* [1936], although the heroine of the latter story chose Bulldog Drummond as her model.

Alongside this development of adventure stories in a home setting came a sudden and marked improvement in the quality of 'exotic' adventure stories. This was to some extent the result of a deliberate policy of Basil Blackwell, who commissioned some of the most promising of young writers – not for the most part previously associated with children's books – to contribute to two new series, 'Tales of Action' and 'Tales of Two Worlds'. Some of these books had period settings, like Philip Lindsay's *Knights at Bay* [1933], and Cecil Day Lewis's *Dick Willoughby* [1933] and, from America, Stephen W. Meader's *Who Rides in the Dark?* [1938]. Adrian Alington's *The Boy King* [1935] used the conventional materials of romantic adventure with individual effect. A superb sea-story by L. A. G. Strong, *Fortnight South of Skye* [1934] and Rex Warner's *The Kite* [1936] were the best of the series; the latter, using a modern setting and concerning itself with the drug traffic in Egypt, was a surprising book for children to meet in the 'thirties. It was almost alone in its concern with international social problems.

Not all adventure stories were of this kind. The Breretons, Westermans and Strangs continued to be read and their ranks were joined by

a phenomenal newcomer, W. E. Johns, whose *Spy Fliers* appeared in
1933. The creator of Biggles (Worralls came along during the Second
World War) belonged, in technique, material and outlook, to the old
tradition. His swift mindless stories at once enjoyed great popularity.
There was more in L. E. O. Charlton's *The Secret Aerodrome* [1933] and
Near East Adventure [1934]; the author had expert knowledge of
aviation and a certain simple zest in writing.

There was other material for popular adventure besides war and the
aftermath of war. One of the veterans, Harold Avery, rose right out
of his class in a story of Captain Scott's last expedition, *No Surrender*
[1933] with Rowland Hilder's fine pictures. Herbert Best, who had
contributed to Basil Blackwell's 'Tales of Two Worlds', turned to
Africa in a remarkably perceptive book *Garram the Hunter* [1935]. This,
superficially at least, belonged to popular fiction. J. S. Phillips, in
South Sea Adventure [1936] and *Malay Adventure* [1937], was more concerned with the documentary aspect of the exotic scene, and this was
more strongly pronounced in *Coconut Island* [1936]. In this Robert
Gibbings matched his wood-engravings with a text of exquisite
simplicity in a tale of the South Seas. So contrived a work of art might
seem destined to a *succes d'estime*. In fact *Coconut Island* has proved to
have an enduring quality; it has outlived all its contemporaries among
the stories of exotic adventure.

(vi) *Families – from One End Street and Elsewhere*

Children's literature, like the novel, was middle-class in origin and
tenaciously faithful to its origins. The poor came often into Victorian
stories, as an object of charity and as an awful warning. There could
have been no Ministering Children without them. They were of no
interest in themselves. Even in their most depressed 'treasure-seeking'
days there was never any doubt of the social standing of the Bastables.
True, Dicky Harding lived as a slum child in the slums, but this served
only to emphasise the magnitude of his translation to be Lord Arden.
By 1935 English children's books seemed firmly middle-class and likely
to continue so; the writers were of that class and so were most of the
readers. It comes as a shock to re-read *Emil* and to realise how, by
contrast, the German book shows a quite unselfconscious classlessness.

In the days of the Depression, Eve Garnett was an art student in
London. She took to walking around the back streets and to drawing
the ill-clothed and under-fed children she saw. Accurate observation
and social conscience made her first an artist, then a writer. *The Family*

from One End Street was originally a social document, a criticism of the conditions which produced poverty, but somewhere in the writing criticism was lost and humour took charge. The result was a book which remains unique in Britain, a picture of working-class people drawn from the life. Eve Garnett made her family funny without inviting condescension; she made them sympathetic without inviting sympathy. The Ruggles of One End Street were in fact interesting, useful people in their own right. The simple adventures sprang from their personalities and their environment; few stories had ever been so little 'invented'. There was the same careful truthfulness in the author's illustrations; these were more than commonly integrated with the text and indeed had been drawn first.

The originality and truthfulness of *The Family from One End Street* won Eve Garnett a Carnegie Medal, and the book has continued to be enjoyed and admired ever since 1937. It had no immediate imitators and the other contemporary stories of family life were almost all strictly middle-class. The exception was Eleanor Graham's *The Children who Lived in a Barn* [1938], a story of poverty and hardship in a rural setting which owed something to Ransome in its emphasis on resourcefulness, and more to the author's own fine critical sense and her insistence on facing difficulties.

With Grace James' *John and Mary* [1935] social problems were forgotten again. Kitty Barne, on the other hand, was well aware of the social order of the 'thirties and if she chose to write mostly of middle-class children she showed them in their contemporary setting. There was a warm homeliness in *Family Footlights* [1939] and deeper understanding in *She shall have music* [1938], the most successful of her books in which she showed how musical ability – she was a fine musician herself – made its way in the face of extreme difficulties and discouragements. There was some understanding, as well as sharp observation, in Kit Higson's *Hundreds and Thousands* [1939], a story of a lively, good-humoured family which might have achieved distinction had its social ethics been less confused. Some of the most satisfying of these family stories were those of Monica Redlich. *Jam Tomorrow* [1937] was a gentle, thoughtful story of a country rectory. *Five Farthings* [1939], superbly illustrated by Rowland Hilder, was a story about London. The Farthings, an exceptionally nice family, went to live in the City of London, literally under the shadow of St. Paul's. London was the principal character in a story which dealt quietly and intelligently with the problems of growing up. Vivien, going to work in a publishing house, discovering the wonder of Wren's architecture, learning the ecstacy of first love, was a most appealing heroine. This was highly competent, professional novel writing. So was Howard Spring's in *Tumbledown Dick* [1939], a brilliant *tour-de-force* which defies classification. Spring who had showed, in his autobiographical fragment *Heaven Lies About Us*, how clearly he remembered the events and sensations of his Manchester childhood, was potentially one of the finest of all writers for children. Success as a novelist kept him out of this field, but in three books [the earliest was *Darkie and Co.*, 1932] he gave some measure of his power.

In a lively, humorous story *Sampson's Circus* [1936] Howard Spring had shown something of the excitement and hard work of circus life. It was, in a sense, a career-book. The most skilful, sincere and honest writer of this kind – and she was much more besides – was Noel Streatfeild. Noel Streatfeild had turned to writing after a brief career on the stage, and her first book for children was a set of short plays *The Children's Matinee* [1934]. Before this, in an adult novel, *The Whicharts* [1931], were the seeds of her first important book, perhaps her best, for children. *Ballet Shoes* [1936] established her immediately as a major writer for children. A story about three orphan children adopted by an absent-minded professor, it showed a profound understanding of child behaviour and a rare concern for accuracy in the factual background. What gave the books its enduring quality was its warm, strong tenderness. The three Fossils were characters who exist in their own right. Noel Streatfeild was too wise and industrious to adopt the soft option of a sequel, but she could not prevent the Fossils creeping back into later stories. The recurrent theme of Noel Streatfeild's writing is the virtue and the necessity of hard work; it was implicit in *Ballet Shoes* and was the very heart of *The Circus is Coming* which won the Carnegie Medal in 1938. Nothing ever came easy to her heroes and heroines. She showed in precise detail the stages of progress towards success and the rewards, in terms of self-respect, of success. Hers were, almost in Victorian terms, 'moral' and 'success' stories, but the moral was not imposed on a story but came from the heart of the writer.

Noel Streatfeild became a writer of career stories almost by accident. Helen D. Boyleston was one by vocation. The first of the American 'Sue Barton' books appeared in England in 1939, and a long succession followed. They gave a colourful but honest picture of a nurse's life in the States, and by their care for authenticity as much as by their romance they set the pattern for the 'machine-made' career book of the 'fifties. Meanwhile two English examples had shown in different ways how authentic information about work might be given in terms of an interesting story: Evelyn Eaton's *John, Film Star* [1937], surprisingly set in France, and Arnold Haskell's *Felicity Dances* [1937].

(vii) *At Home Abroad*

The influx of foreign children's books during the 'thirties has already been noted. This was an age of curiosity, of an interest in the ways of other people. For children at least the negroes no longer began at Calais. This new cosmopolitan was mirrored in books imported from abroad as well as in those written in England to interpret the life of other nations.

The classic story of this kind was *Dobry*. Monica Shannon's book which won the Newbery Medal in 1935 was published in England in the following year. (It has recently been reissued.) The author, an American of Irish origin, made her way most wonderfully into the mind of a Bulgarian peasant boy. Dobry might appear to be exceptional in that he wanted to become an artist, but the author showed how he was in fact merely trying to give physical form to the poetry of nature as primitive people saw it. The book was perhaps a little overcharged with meaning; there was certainly great beauty in grandfather's vision of the renewing earth. Something of the same peasant poetry translated into slightly sophisticated terms was to be found in Kate Seredy's story of her native Hungary *The Good Master* [1937] with the author's own exquisite pictures.

If the Americans sometimes, like this, gave words to emotions which the English prefer unstated, they could also be most beautifully simple, particularly when they wrote not of their European origins but of their own rural and small-town life. Elizabeth Enright's Garnet in *Thimble Summer* [1939] was as American as Huck Finn. There was a fine frankness and spiritual toughness in a story which grew naturally without any invention on the author's part.

Just as American, and just as successful, was Rachel Field's *Hitty* [1932], which was superficially just a doll-story but which was the story, too, of a century of national development. Elizabeth Coatsworth, too, created the atmosphere of New England in *Alice All-by-Herself* [1938].

There was nothing especially Canadian about Muriel Dennison's Susannah [*Susannah of the Mounties*, 1938] who was like self-willed little girls the world over. Stephen Meader, in *Lumberjack* [1934] and *Trap-lines North* [1936] brought vividly to life the hardness of the Northern wilds.

As a Mission Teacher the American Elizabeth Foreman Lewis was aware at first hand of the effects of revolution in China. In *Yung Fu of the Upper Yangtse* [1934] and perhaps even more in *Ho-Ming, Girl of New China* [1935] she recorded her faith in the fundamental greatness of the Chinese and their powers of endurance and recovery, and her recognition of their essential kinship with other people.

The European books were quieter and less emotional. Averill Demuth's *Trudi and Hansel* [1938] a gentle picture of country life in Germany; Karin Michaelis's Danish *Bibi* [1933] in a beautiful translation by Rose Fyleman; above all Ninke van Hichtum's *Afke's Ten*, a slow, rich and humorous story of a large Dutch family; these conveyed the essential atmosphere of their countries. But the outsider's view was also interesting. Marjorie Fischer's *Street Fair* [1935], with a French setting, and still more her *Palaces on Monday* [1937], a sharply defined picture of life in Soviet Russia, had the advantage of an intelligent, sympathetic and critical approach.

(viii) *Experiments in Information*

In 1932 *An Outline for Boys and Girls and their Parents* was published by Victor Gollancz. This was in its way as big an event as the publication of *Swallows and Amazons* and as influential. Ransome had had his precursors. There had been nothing like the *Outline*. It was not an encyclopaedia but a critical stock-taking of contemporary knowledge. It was up-to-date; indeed it presented the advanced thought in each of its subjects. It was written for intelligent people of all ages. The simplification lay in the way in which difficult concepts were presented by means of illustration and example, not in an artificial restriction of language or an avoidance of complexities. For the first time in factual literature children were treated as sensible, responsible beings; the book assumed that they would be interested in all aspects of knowledge, the origins of life, the arts of government, and communication through the arts. The editor, Naomi Mitchison, had assembled a team of experts, among them Wystan Auden who "writes poetry and teaches", a "young economist who lectures at London University" called Hugh Gaitskell, and Richard Hughes writing, surprisingly, about physics, astronomy and mathematics, and seeing them "newly and excitingly and in a way that connects them with the rest of life". These words summed up the whole purpose of the *Outline*. The book never preached or lectured; above all it encouraged the reader to think for himself.

The *Outline* pointed to one way of development for informative books for children, by feeding curiosity about the world around. Science had a wider application than the school laboratory. This was emphasised in a book by two scientists of the first rank, E. N. da C. Andrade and Julian Huxley, in their book *Simple Science* [1934]. This and its successor *More Simple Science* [1935] brought difficult scientific ideas to life more vividly than any part of the *Outline*. Sir James Jeans' Royal Institution lectures *Through Space and Time* [1934] were equally striking simplifications of modern astronomical knowledge and theory. Doris L. Mackinnon applied similar methods to zoology in *The Animals' World* [1936], and John Langdon-Davis dealt with highly complex new researches in *Inside the Atom* [1934].

All these were the work of highly qualified scientists who happened to be also brilliantly successful at exposition. Their books made considerable demands on the reader; they were addressed to children and to intelligent citizens of any age. By contrast, a book like C. F. Oddie's *The Night School of the Learned Swan* [1933], which set out to introduce physics to children, seemed naïve. T. J. S. Rowlands' first picture-book *Living Things for Lively Youngsters* [1933] had a more modest range and a disarming informality, the work of a competent amateur; it offered a sharp contrast to the highly professional books (from the United States) of Raymond C. Ditmars with their fine illustrations and expansive format. *The Book of Zoography* [1935] introduced a distinguished series. Other interesting experiments in the presentation of factual information came from the U.S.S.R. M. Ilin's books were physically unimpressive, but he was unobtrusively successful in illustrating the idea of time in *What Time is it?* [1932] and light in *Turning Night into Day* [1937]. Eleanor Doorly chose to expound scientific ideas in terms of biography; her brief lives of Fabre, Pasteur and Madame Curie were written with quiet sincerity and sound scientific judgment.

The Gollancz *Outline* laid strong emphasis on sociology. Economic and political crises, national and international, claimed the reluctant interest of adult readers of the newspaper and of the politico-economist books which were appearing in large numbers for the first time. Much of this interest filtered through to children, some of whom were being introduced to a new classroom subject, Civics. H. C. Knapp-Fisher's *Outline of World History for Boys and Girls* [1931] was startlingly different from the old kinds of history-books with their chronicles of unexplained warfare. In *The Modern World* [1933] and *The World of Man for Boys and Girls* [1939] the same author applied his theories of history to an examination of sociology. Meanwhile I. O. Evans had published *The Junior Outline of History* [1932] in which he digested H. G. Wells for young stomachs. One of the most interesting books of the period was *Pollycon* [1933] in which E. F. Stucley attempted to explain the principles of political economy to children much younger than those for whom the *Outline* was designed. The author's anecdotes illustrating cheques, bills of exchange and the like were as good as Hugh Chesterman's amusing illustrations, but she got into difficulties – as how could she not? – in dealing with controversial issues. *Pollycon* demonstrated the hazards of over-simplification. Kathleen Gibbard was less amusing and more impartial; her *Young Citizens* [1935] and *Citizenship through the Newspaper* [1939] were admirable sober introductions. Amabel Williams-Ellis, who, in *What Shall I Be?* [1933] had managed to convey some general truths in a topical book on careers, joined with F. J. Fisher in an admirable *History of English Life* [1936] which, without eccentricity, abandoned the conventions of historical writing in favour of a history of the lives of ordinary people and the social, economic and political forces which played upon them.

Some excellent new series were initiated by publishers. The Cambridge University Press's 'British Institution' series [*G.P.O.* by E. T.

Crutchley, 1938] was extremely practical and avoided over-simplification; so did Oxford's 'Pageant of Progress' [*Engines Today* by John Harrison, 1936], which achieved simplicity by a skilled selection of material. Oxford's 'World Goes By' series was distinguished by a handsome picture-book style format, but in a book like A. C. Hardy's *Ships* [1939] the text did not rise to the standard of Lewis Lupton's fine drawing. Black's 'How and Why' and Nelson's 'Horizon Books' were more conventional but not much less effective. Perhaps the most interesting books in series were the 'Chameleon Books' started by Oxford University Press in 1938. These were very small and cheap, but presented with great style and ranging over a variety of subjects. They were particularly valuable as an elegant and inexpensive vehicle for modern verse.

Although conventionally instructive books continued to appear, there was a considerable emphasis on informality. Geoffrey Holme in *The Children's Art Book* [1937] showed how to look for qualities of composition and draughtsmanship alike in an Old Master and a modern lithograph and kept up a disarmingly good-humoured flow of conversation. Ernest La Prade's *Alice in Orchestra Land* [1934] introduced the instruments of the orchestra in a fantastic vein which stopped a little this side of whimsy; Malcolm Sargent stood sponsor to the book and vouched for its authenticity. G. Branwell Evens brought the teeming life of the countryside into focus in his *Romany in the Country* [1932], and F. Fraser Darling, with fine engravings by C. F. Tunnicliffe and equally good photographs, showed the workaday aspects of the country in *The Seasons and the Farmer* [1939]. From America the first of Opal Wheeler and Sybil Deucher's introductions to the great musicians – *Joseph Haydn, the Merry Peasant* – blended agreeably anecdote and musical example. The most distinguished of all informal introductions came, too, from America, Van Loon's *The Arts of Mankind*, a book of masterly comprehensiveness and supreme simplicity, and with the author's illustrations conveying in a single scribble the essence of Rembrandt or Van Gogh. In books like this, author and reader shared in a creative experience.

(ix) *Illustration in the 'thirties*

Although important work continued to be done by artists of the 'colour-plate' school like Rackham and Charles Folkard, the native trend in illustrations was towards a closer integration of picture and text. Most artists worked, not altogether for reasons of economy, in

black-and-white, finding satisfaction in submission to the discipline of
the printed page.

Some of the most interesting work was by artists who had encountered either the teaching or the tradition of Edmund J. Sullivan at
Goldsmiths' College. There were marked common features in at any
rate the earlier work of Rowland Hilder and C. Walter Hodges, both
of whom studied under Sullivan, and Jack Matthew whose teacher at
Goldsmiths' was Hilder. All three were first-rate draughtsmen and
sound traditional designers; all showed a fondness for using bold masses
of white and black which was reminiscent of Sullivan.

Another group of artists showed signs of their common training at
the Central School of Arts and Crafts. If Sullivan's students looked to
the nineteenth (and eighteenth) century tradition, these were boldly
modern and resourceful in the use of new techniques. They were also
individual, and it is not difficult to see the liberating influence of the
Central School's teaching in work as excellent and varied as that of
Clarke Hutton, Pearl Binder, Marcia Lane-Foster, Jocelyn Crowe and
the Morton-Sales. John and Isabel Morton-Sale were among the
outstandingly successful illustrators of the period. Their range was
narrow and they sometimes leaned uncomfortably in the direction of
sentimentality – an effect perhaps of their magazine-work; but they
happily captured the gentle and homely fantasy of Eleanor Farjeon's
verse as well as the tougher spirit of John Buchan's *Magic Walking
Stick* [1932].

The vogue for wood-engraving was a by-product of the private
presses which flourished in the 'thirties. The appeal to children of this
technique was always rather limited, but the fine artistic integrity
behind much careful and charming work was beyond question. Among
older artists, Eric Fitch Daglish continued his exact work in books of
nature-study. Perhaps the most immediately enjoyable work was done
by Cecily Englefield in a series of amusing picture-books for which she
provided the text. The work of the highest artistic quality came from
Robert Gibbings, Gwen Raverat and Clare Leighton. Gibbings was a
Private-Press man who had perfected a technique of great versatility
and produced results of masterly simplicity. His finest work at this
time was in a book on the borderline between adult and children's
literature, Helen Waddell's translations *Beasts and Saints* [1934]; here
his work was free of fussiness and used the bold line and the large white
areas of early woodcuts. Gwen Raverat, a grand-daughter of Darwin
and an artist of poetic sensibility, did some exquisite and minute work

illustrating Andersen and for Grahame's *Cambridge Book of Poetry for Children*, and Eleanor Farjeon's *Over the Garden Wall* [both 1933]. Clare Leighton, who preferred to work on a much larger scale, was more successful in conveying the tragic emotions of adult literature, in Hardy or Emily Brönte; she was altogether too strong for Eleanor Farjeon's *Perkin the Pedlar* [1932] and even perhaps for her own *Musical Box* [1936].

A cheaper technique which produced somewhat similar results to wood-engraving became popular at this time. This was scraper-board, which Rex Whistler used in his exquisite Andersen drawings, and of which C. F. Tunnicliffe became an outstanding master. It might be just to rate Whistler's illustrations to Walter de la Mare's *The Lord Fish* [1933] even higher than his Andersen pictures. They were fewer and narrower in range, but he caught the tender melancholy of De la Mare's world to perfection.

Much good work was done in two traditional veins, the humorous and the naturalistic. Among humorous artists, the 'Punch' school, one might say, the outstanding figure was Ernest H. Shepard and with him might be put J. H. Dowd, who was particularly happy at children, and Steven Spurrier, whose drawings for *Tumbledown Dick* [1939] and incomplete sketches for Noel Streatfeild's *The Circus is Coming* were of high quality. Contrasted with these was the drawing of Nicolas Bentley, seen in Hugh E. Wright's *There was a Moon* [1934], which with its clean line and sharply satirical outlook seemed to belong to 'Lilliput' rather than to 'Punch'.

Much of the best of the naturalistic drawing was in the Junior Country Life Library, particularly in work by Lionel Edwards and Vernon Stokes and Cynthia Harnett. Anne Bullen's horses, and D. L. Mays' and Ruth Gervis's figures were admirable. Stuart Tresilian's drawings for Kipling's 'Mowgli' stories had drama and atmosphere.

Some experiments were made in the imaginative use of photography in illustration. This had previously been limited in children's books almost entirely to factual books. An attempt to illustrate W. W. Tarn's *Treasure of the Isle of Mist* with photographs of Skye in 1938 was unsatisfactory, partly because the photographs themselves were not of high quality. Books by Ylla [*Big and Little*, 1938] and Harold Burdekin [*The Secret*, 1938] were of the highest technical excellence, but they were little more than picture-books with an accompanying text. The problem of integrating text and photographs in a closely knit whole remained unsolved.

CHAPTER 6

CHILDREN'S BOOKS IN THE SECOND WORLD WAR

THE decade before the outbreak of war in 1939 had been an exciting period, with interesting experiments, much fine writing, stimulating influences from abroad, a growing awareness of standards in children's books among teachers, librarians and parents. The first and most obvious effect of the war was a sharp reduction in the number of new children's books published. Authors, illustrators, printers and publishers all had other things to do; there was a grave shortage of labour and materials, particularly paper. Then in the London Blitz of 29th December 1940 vast quantities of books, blocks, irreplaceable drawings and publishers' records went up in flames in the traditional centre of publishing around St. Pauls. The Blitz was no critic; classics and 'Rewards' suffered alike. Indeed the 'Reward' trade suffered a blow from which it has never fully recovered. Many good books which were destroyed in this holocaust have never been reprinted. A particularly serious result was the lack during the war years, and for several years afterwards, of editions of children's classics. Books by E. Nesbit, Beatrix Potter and Kipling acquired a most undesired rarity value. Ironically the serviceman found in cities overseas a generous supply of the books for which readers looked in vain in British bookshops.

As the war went on and supplies became scarcer, prices rose and physical standards were lowered. A large amount of many publishers' quota of paper was squandered on trivial books long since forgotten. Much of what was written was conventional in subject and manner; the best minds were occupied elsewhere. Twice no Carnegie Medal was awarded, and it might be argued that on some other occasions the selection committee lowered its sights. It was perhaps remarkable that worth-while books were published at all. The editor of *Junior Bookshelf*, after a period of despondency when he announced that the review would close down for the duration, was persuaded to resume publication, and in the ensuing years an edition reduced in size but not barren of content appeared remarkably regularly.

The children were the first casualties of the war. Before the formal declaration was made, many thousands of children had begun their journey from crowded cities to the apparent safety of the country. Evacuation was a kind of tragi-comic picnic. As a policy it failed because so many children returned home before the bombs began to fall. It was a memorable experience for everyone, and for a few, like Fred in Kitty Barne's *Visitors from London* [1940], it was a turning-point in life. *Visitors from London* was a topical winner of the Carnegie Medal. By no means the author's best book, it was an accurate documentary of the first period, as Mary Treadgold's *We Couldn't Leave Dinah* [1941] was of the second phase of the war. P. L. Travers, the creator of Mary Poppins, also chose to write about evacuation, but *I go by sea, I go by land* [1941] dealt with the far more serious dilemma of children evacuated to America.

Kitty Barne used the conventions of the adventure story in two other books with a war-time setting: *We'll Meet in England* [1946], about an escape from occupied Norway, and *In the Same Boat* [1945] a thriller which had at its core a genuine problem of international relations. In *The Vedor Sampler* [1944] Audrey Clark wrote sensitively about the plight of Czechoslovakia under the Nazi occupation.

The Home Front provided plenty of material for stories. An attractive book for younger children, illustrated by the Czech artist Walter Trier who had first become noticed for his illustrations to *Emil*, was Elinor Mordaunt's *Blitz Kids* [1941], which had some honest observation. The most sincere naturalistic writing was by Lorna Lewis, in *Tea and Hot Bombs* [1943] and *Feud in the Factory* [1944]. Both these stories dealt with the less glamorous aspects of life on the fringe of the war effort, and showed young people doing unfamiliar and often unpleasant jobs and getting from the experience a share of excitement and fun.

The war gave new vitality to the worn formulae of the 'thriller'. In *The Children of Primrose Lane* [1941] Noel Streatfeild gave a topical colouring to a conventional, but characteristically competent, story of children and spies. Spies even penetrated, not perhaps for the first time, the walls of the girls' school, in, for example, *Nancy Calls the Tune* [1944] in which Dorita Fairlie Bruce shows, with some humour and good spirits, a young girl's involvement in secret service activities.

The Blue-coated Heron [1944] too was a war story. Clare Collas's story was a sequel to two earlier books about talking animals and their adventures with children. *The Blue-coated Heron* was a little less fantastic, a comic adventure-story with a little basic fantasy. The events which lead to the award at Buckingham Palace of the Order of the

Blue-coated Heron to Jacob the Cat and Mr. Hawkins the parrot have their share of excitement and high comedy; and the realistic portraits of the child and adult characters, beautifully realised in Dod Procter's illustrations, give a touchstone of normality to keep the fantasy in proportion. The references to the war are direct in this book. In two other war-time fantasies no mention was made of the war, but *After Bath* and *The Wind on the Moon* were nevertheless the most important direct products of the war.

In *After Bath* [1945] Vaughan Wilkins wrote a comic fantasy which was not allegorical but which, like the best fantasies, had allegorical elements. It was a book which seemed to have begun as an improvised narrative to be told, serial-fashion, 'after bath', and in its early chapters it had too much of the topicality and the private jokes which resulted from this informal origin. Almost in spite of himself the author began to find richer meaning in his story which rose to heights of excitement and emotion. The climax was in the grand manner. The blending of farce and seriousness was not always successful; but the basic theme was timeless and noble, dealing as it did with the rewards of courage and the necessity for sacrifice. Occasionally absurd, occasionally horrifying, *After Bath* had an untidy, episodic plot and some lapses in taste, but its grandeur of conception and richness of invention put it among the most interesting and imaginative productions of Britain during the war. *The Wind on the Moon* [1944] was another farcical comedy, originally improvised, which turned serious. Eric Linklater has described how he made up the story to placate two angry daughters; the first half of the story was of this kind, with its bold characterisation and fantastic invention of improbabilities. In the second half, the parallels between Count Hulagu Bloot's Bombardy and Hitler's Germany became clear, and a note of seriousness and even tragedy crept into the story. *The Wind on the Moon* was a less imaginative fantasy than *After Bath;* the accomplished, professional writing lifted it into a class of its own and made it an inevitable choice for the Carnegie Medal.

Only one book provided a stronger comment on the war, and this came from the United States. *Johnny Tremain* was an historical novel looking at a scene vastly different from Hitler's Europe, but Esther Forbes found lessons for the twentieth, and any other, century in the problems of New England on the brink of the War of Independence. *Johnny Tremain* won the Newbery Medal, but the first English edition in 1944 attracted little attention. The better designed edition of 1958 brought its remarkable qualities out into the light. It was a beautifully written story, viewing a crisis in world history through the eyes of a complex, difficult, intelligent boy. There was no anachronism in the story, but James Otis, talking to the Boston rebels of 1773, summarised the war aims of 1943 that "we fight, we die . . . only that a man may stand up".

Most of the talented refugees from Nazism used Britain merely as a spring-board for America. However, 'Bettina' [Bettina Ehrlich] settled in London from Austria and published her first book here in 1943. This was *Poo-Tse the Water Tortoise*, which was followed by the more characteristic *Cocolo* in 1945. More immediate results were achieved by the Polish artists, Jan Lewitt and George Him, who settled in England. Each was a distinguished artist in his own right, but they worked so successfully in partnership that 'Lewitt-Him' became the symbol of a singular excellence. *Locomotive*, published in England by the Minerva Press in 1939, was a major landmark in the history of the picture-book. Four poems by the Polish writer J. Tuwin, indifferently good in translation, sprang into life in pictures of startling colour and bold, vigorous design. *The Football's Revolt* [1939], with a text by the artists, showed a vein of broad comedy which characterised the later books *Blue Peter* and *Five Silly Cats* [both 1942]. In *The Little Red Engine Gets a Name* [1942], to Diana Ross's text, they were closer to their original style, in which humour was softened with a poetic appreciation of natural beauty. Lewitt-Him provided a powerful stimulus to contemporary illustration, and their influence was to be seen widely, not only in the obvious, and competent, imitation with which Leslie Wood continued the 'Little Red Engine' stories in 1945 with *The Story of the Little Red Engine*.

As the war continued, books were introduced not only from the United States but also from Russia. M. Bulatov's *The Wild Goose* was a characteristic Russian picture-book which appeared in 1944. The American picture-books were more immediately interesting. (An exhibition of American picture-books at Chaucer House in November, 1944, achieved publicity on a national scale.) Holling Clancy Holling was as American as his name. In *Paddle-to-the-Sea* [1941] and *Tree in the Trail* [1942] he captured the beauty of wild nature with great fidelity. The cosmopolitan talents of William Pene du Bois were in sharp contrast. *The Great Geppy* [1942] and *Elizabeth the Cow Ghost* [1944] had the precision of the serious absurdity which were characteristics of this brilliant young artist. In *Mike Mulligan and his Steam Shovel* [1942] Virginia Lee Burton appeared first before a British audience; this was followed in 1944 by *Choo Choo*. Fine design and colour gave distinction to these amusing stories of machines with personality. Kurt Wiese's drawings for *The Ferryman* [1943], a folk-tale told by Claire Huchet Bishop, were economical and beautifully matched to the serio-comical tone of the story. Perhaps the most charming, and American, of these war-time picture-books was the Caldecott winner *Make Way for Duckling* [1944], which used with restraint and quiet humour an actual incident in Boston; Robert McClosky's story and pictures were perfectly balanced.

Not all the best of the war-time picture-books were importations. In 1940 the first Puffin Picture Books appeared under the editorship of Noel Carrington. These paper-backed books, originally costing 6d. each, set new standards in book design. Using offset lithography the publisher was able to achieve both harmony of text and picture and very fine colour-printing at a low cost. The first titles in the series were topical war books, of no great artistic interest, but in the second year of their publication Puffins started the series of nature-books which were to be among their highest achievements. Two books by S. R. Badmin, *Village and Town* [1942] and *Trees in Britain* [1943] were of the greatest beauty and accuracy. The series was avowedly educational. In another war-time series of cheap books, less successful but of great interest, were those "beautiful little scraps of paper", the Chatto and Windus Midget Books.

The doyen of English illustrators, Edward Ardizzone, was an official war artist with no time for original picture-books, although 'Little Tim' appeared in wartime austerity in 1944. The war provided a few new symbols like Enid Marx's *Bulgy the Barrage Balloon* [1941], but most artists, like Harold Jones in *The Visit to the Farm* [1941], aimed at time-lessness rather than topicality. Among young illustrators, Jack Townend showed the influence, or the common inspiration, of Lewitt-Him. *A Railway A.B.C.* [1942] and still more *Ben* [1944] showed a fine mastery of colour and design, as well as a strong sense of humour. Hilary Stebbing too belonged to the Lewitt-Him school, if in *Maggie the Streamlined Taxi* [1943] she lacked some of their virtuosity and their fine taste. Kathleen Hale escaped from Orlando the Marmalade Cat to invent an equally appealing heroine *Henrietta the Faithful Hen* [1943], a large book which showed few signs of the ravages of war. Both this and Hilary Stebbing's book were published by Transatlantic Arts, for which Noel Carrington was the designer. A new artist, Cam [Barbara Campbell] owed too much to Disney, but her richly decorated work in

Barbara Lamb[1944] and *Buttercup Fairy* [1945] had its share of sentiment and humour. Ursula Moray Williams' *The Good Little Christmas Tree* [1943] used a scissor-cut technique with interesting effect. Experiments in the use of photography continued. Margaret Fischer and Henry Rox got fun out of photographing natural objects in unnatural contexts in *Banana Circus*, and in *First Things* Paul Heming used very simple colour photography to make a small child's first guide to the world around him. Using no technique other than that of good drawing, V. H. Drummond told, in *Mrs. Easter's Parasol* [1944], a story of London's streets and parks in which keen observation and a rich sense of absurdity produced a most satisfying harmony.

Just a year after the beginning of Puffin Picture Books, Penguin Books started a new series of Puffin Story Books. These were not at first original books, but books mostly of the past twenty years. The editor was Eleanor Graham, whose fine standards and catholic appreciation gave the series an unmistakable authority.

One of the best imaginative books was a direct product of the war. At the beginning of the war Richard Hughes found himself acting as host to a party of Lancashire children in his Welsh home. For their amusement he told the stories published in 1940 as *Don't Blame Me!* In their fantastic humour, their exquisite and informal writing, above all in their blending of magic and contemporary commonplaces, these tales marked an advance on the author's previous *Spider's Palace*. Not many of the fantastic stories of the war years were of this quality. In 1940 Alison Uttley's Sam Pig stories – *Tales of Four Pigs and Brock the Badger* – appeared, and she published several other attractive collections during the war without once achieving the perfection of which she seemed capable. Pleasant books by Susan Tweedsmuir, Barbara Hastings and Dorothy Ann Lovell maintained a good standard. Diana Ross began to show promise of fine writing and invention; her *Nursery Tales* [1944] had the aural and rhythmic interest which came of being written for broadcasting. R. W. Hatch's *The Curious Lobster's Island* [1940] and Beverley Nichols' *The Tree that Sat Down* [1945] had a sense of style and some fantastic humour. W. C. Dickinson's *Borrobil* [1944] was closer to the British tradition of fantasy. In *Poo Poo and the Dragons* [1942] C. S. Forester, aided by superb drawings by Robert Lawson, came nearer than most successful adult writers to finding a comic formula acceptable to children. Elizabeth Gorell's bear-books [*Bitty and the Bears*, 1942, and *Stubbington Manor*, 1943] had some individual quality as well as some Pooh-like humour. In two books of folk-tales Joan Grant enriched her material with fine writing, more successfully in *The Scarlet Fish* [1942].

The most distinguished fantasy of the war years was *The Little Grey Men* [1943]. The author, B.B. [D. J. Watkins-Pitchford], was a country-man and an artist, an admirable combination in the writer of a book which, in terms of fantasy, sought to capture the beauty and the wonder of an English year. He chose an unspectacular part of the Midland countryside for his setting and, by making his heroes the last gnomes of England, he was able to show a close-up of wild creatures and the hazardous life they live. *The Little Grey Men* was a little better in con-ception than in execution. The author had too pedestrian a style for his material. In integrity, in authoritative observation, and in the rough poetry of the idea, this was a book of great distinction, timely and timeless.

It was not the best time for poetry; only Eleanor Farjeon publishing work of original interest. In *Cherrystones* [1942] and *The Mulberry Bush* [1945] she was in her happiest vein in two series of linked rhymes. In 1941 Walter de la Mare published some verses, mostly dating back to the days of *Peacock Pie*, which provided a delightful glimpse into the past. *Bells and Grass* had no verses as good as De la Mare's best, but they ranged wide and had the familiar magic of word and idea. An artist then working on aircraft design but destined to world fame as a comic draughtsman, Rowland Emett, provided illustrations which matched the poet's mysticism as well as his grotesque comedy. In 1944 De la Mare's verses for children were issued in a collected edition.

Two unusual books came from France during the war. Andrê Maurois's *Fattypuffs and Thinifers* [1941] was a comic fantasy full of exact circumstantial detail; perhaps a little too cerebral to make a successful story for young children. *The Little Prince* [1945] was by that extraordinary warrior-mystic Antoine de Saint-Exupéry. This delicate poetical fantasy belongs to the borderland between children's and adult literature. But for its success with individual children, one might think that it was a book *about* childhood.

Shortages of paper and of time reduced the output of most writers, but not Enid Blyton. During the four years 1942-45, lean years generally, sixty-seven of her books were published. (In the same period there were two books by Noel Streatfeild, one a reprint, and one by Arthur Ransome, or, to make a less exalted comparison, seven by Malcolm Saville). These included fairy tales, stories retold from Uncle Remus and the Bible, country stories, mysteries, school stories, annuals, adventures, stories of 'naughty children'. Only W. E. Johns and Malcolm Saville competed with her for popular approval, and neither attempted so wide a range. Malcolm Saville, in a series of competent stories, beginning with *Mystery at Witchend* [1943], made a bid to become the poor child's Arthur Ransome. Ransome himself approached the end of his matchless series in *The Picts and the Martyrs* [1943] which returned to the scene of the first stories with some of the old high spirits and a deepening awareness of responsibility. Together with their creator the Swallows, the Amazons and the Ds were growing older. Meanwhile several authors had applied the Ransome formula to subjects of their own. Aubrey de Selincourt's first story, *Family Afloat*, appeared in 1940, and several others, all characterised by a keen concern with technical details of sailing, followed. David Severn's *Rick Afire* [1942] and later stories were landsman's tales which were concerned with problems of human behaviour. Virginia Pye's family stories recalled Noel Streatfeild rather than Ransome; her sharp sense of humour gave an individual quality to *Red Letter Holiday* [1940]. Elizabeth Kyle's novels, *Vanishing Island* [1942] and *Holly Hotel* [1945] offer a Scottish counterpart, less amusing but perhaps more thoughtful, to the stories of the Price family. E. H. Young's *Caravan Island* [1940] and *River Holiday* [1942] were highly competent professional work owing nothing to another writer, although they found an audience among admirers of Ransome.

The most interesting of the open-air books was B.B.'s *Brendon Chase* [1944]. The country setting and the careful detail were reminiscent of Ransome, but this story of two truant boys living wild in the woods had an amoral quality which belonged rather to *Bevis*. B.B. made the irresponsible life of *Brendon Chase* so appealing that he was forced conscientiously to point out throughout the story that this was a story of the past and that it could not happen again. Few books have conveyed so successfully the smell of fresh air and the feel of grass and bracken.

Among animals stories two from America, Mary O'Hara's *My Friend Flicka* [1943] and Eric Knight's *Lassie-Come-Home* [1942] with an English setting, betrayed by their extreme emotionalism that they were really books for adults. The quiet objective writing of Richard Church in *A Squirrel Called Rufus* [1941] was for adults and children alike; so were John Skeaping's masterly crayon drawings.

The school story seemed an anachronism in the world of 1941. The charm of Pamela Brown's *The Swish of the Curtain* [1941] derived partly from the fact that the author was herself a schoolgirl, partly from the interest of the amateur-acting theme, mostly from the vigorous characterisation. In the first of an Oxford University Press series of 'Career Books', *Students at Queens* [1945], J. S. Arey explored conscientiously and not unsympathetically the world of the medical student. The best of the school stories, however, were by L. A. G. Strong, who was capable of injecting new life into the worn-out formula devised so long ago by Talbot Baines Reed. In *Wrong Foot Foremost* [1940] he chose to write about the problems arising from the amalgamation of two public schools with their different traditions. In *Sink or Swim* [1945] he rang the changes on a conventional story by making his hero a boy who was good at his lessons and poor at games. It would never have done for Wodehouse!

Two interesting stories of Ireland appeared in the same year, 1941. Marjorie Dixon's *The King of Fiddles* was vigorously told and animated by a strong anti-British bias. Patricia Lynch also, for almost the only time, let a political note creep into her story in *Fiddler's Quest*. This was her first important book to exclude the supernatural, depending on the magic of the author's style and the poet's freshness of her view of life. This book was full of the beauty of everyday things, even in the slums of Dublin.

The Mystery of Obadiah [1943] was of no great interest for its plot, but Richard Armstrong in it transferred the Ransome integrity and concern with practical detail from the holiday to the workaday world. His choice of an industrial setting was unusual, and he wrote about the Tyneside factory with first-hand authority; what was equally unusual was the manly tone. The writer spoke to boys as responsible equals, showing them, in the framework of a mystery story, the dignity of work and the satisfaction of a job well done.

For the first time since H. G. Wells' early days a writer of literary excellence turned to the scientific fantasy. *Lost Men in the Grass* [1940] had the terrifying commonplace of Wells' best work in this kind, with a quiet precision of expression which was the author's own. The writer appeared under the pseudonym of 'Alan Griff', but in a later edition he was revealed as Donald Suddaby. *Lost Men in the Grass* had the simplest of themes. Three men are suddenly reduced in size to the scale in which the grass makes an almost impenetrable jungle and an insect becomes the most formidable adversary. The author faced the implications of his idea quite ruthlessly.

Two stories of outstanding quality came from America. In 1942

Armstrong Sperry's Newbery prize-winner was published in England under the title *The Boy who was Afraid*. This brief story of a Polynesian boy's courage was a masterpiece of understatement; eschewing all heroics it managed to tell a story of a great heroism and to convey a fine simple philosophy. Doris Gates' *Blue Willow* dealt with poverty in the American rural scene. With obvious truth and great tenderness it drew a picture of hardship redeemed by courage and persistence.

No English historical novel of the war years managed, as had *Johnny Tremain*, to point to a parallel between past and present. Most were content to provide an escape from present realities, into romantic swashbuckling in C. Fox Smith's *The Ship Aground* [1940] or into a past which, by its remoteness, offered a contrast to the hazards of the present. Magdalen King-Hall in *Sturdy Rogue* [1945], and still more E. K. Seth-Smith in *When Shakespeare Lived in Southwark* [1944], gave convincing pictures of Elizabethan life. Marjorie Bowen dealt competently with the French Revolution in *Strangers to Freedom* [1940], and in *The Conqueror* [1945] Margaret Leighton had a set of brilliant miniatures of mediaeval life. The American Newbery Medal winner *Adam of the Road* [1943] by Elizabeth Janet Gray offered a most highly coloured version of the Middle Ages. Much the most interesting historical story was by John Buchan. *The Long Traverse* [1941] was the product both of a lifetime of thought about the meaning of history and of years as Governor-General of Canada. The book was intuitive rather than documented history, but it sought out the origins of a great nation with a mystical intensity which was at once moving and convincing.

Informative books were for the most part unenterprising during the war. A few publishers followed the lead of the Puffin Picture Books in presenting factual material in a brilliant integration of picture and text. Pleiades Books were a leader in book design of this kind. *Balbus* [1944], with text by Oliver Hill and pictures by Hans Tisdall, was a masterly exposition of the art of building; and the same publishers were responsible for Eileen Mayo's *Shells and How They Live* [1944] and *Little Animals of the Countryside* [1945]. Perhaps the most interesting extension of the Puffin idea was Clarke Hutton's *Picture History of Britain* [1945] which covered three thousand years of history in bold colourful drawings and a sound unobtrusive text.

Other non-fictional books were more conventional. Dents started their 'Traveller's Tales' in 1940 with Frank S. Smyth's *The Adventures of a Mountaineer;* these books had a satisfyingly 'grown-up' appearance which appealed to older children, and the writing made reasonable demands on the reader. Dorothy Fisk dealt with the topical science of meteorology competently in *The Sun, the Sky and Kit* [1940], and Mervyn Bruxner, in the same year, published *Letters to a Musical Boy* which without condescending offered a basis for sound appreciation. An outstanding modern poet, C. Day Lewis, provided a handbook to his craft in *Poetry for You* [1944]. This was a contribution to a new view of education as much as a highly entertaining hour or two with a cultivated companion.

The Education Act of 1944 had incalculable implications for publishers, authors and librarians, as well as for the teachers to whom its effects were more immediately apparent. To the publisher it offered a challenge which has still to be fully taken up. It was to produce a new type of reader and to demand a new type of literature. Somehow or other books had to be found for the 'Roaring Boys', and in their search for material for the backward reader, teachers were in danger of forgetting the needs of the eager reader. As the publishing industry adjusted itself to this new demand, a gradual but considerable change in the balance of publishing took place.

CHAPTER 7

RECOVERY

THE years immediately following the war were years of political and economic crises, of chronic shortages, of dissatisfaction and disillusionment. There was general distrust of the past and only a moderate optimism about the future. With this went an urge to experiment.

The shortage of paper and of books continued. The war-time quota system for the supply of paper had encouraged the establishment of new publishing firms and many new publishers continued to appear. Not all of these lasted long, but some, like Peter Lunn, made interesting experiments in design, and others, like John Lehmann, encouraged young and progressive writers.

The war had made nearly a clean sweep of the old 'Rewards' and few were reprinted in the immediate post-war years. In the years 1948–50, for example, the *English Catalogue* records no books by Herbert Strang, Brereton, Evelyn Everett Green or Angela Brazil, one by Harold Avery and seven by Percy F. Westerman. The first five of the post-war years belonged, quantitatively at least, to Enid Blyton. The *English Catalogue* gives her a total score, including reprints, of 183 titles in the years 1946–50, and in 1951 alone 66 titles are recorded. Enid Blyton had been a prolific writer for many years, but these figures were something quite new in children's publishing. They seem likely to remain an all-time record. The books varied greatly in size and content, but at their most considerable they could not perhaps be called very good. Eileen Colwell, reviewing *The Sea of Adventure* in *Junior Bookshelf* in 1948, commented on the plot "What hope has a band of desperate men against four children?" The phenomenal popularity of Enid Blyton was due to some extent to excellent publicity and much more to the painless nature of her writing; in vocabulary and syntax, in plot, ideas, social and moral values, the books contained just what a child was capable of assimilating without effort. If the sole measure of a children's writer were the ability to please children, then Enid Blyton would rank very high indeed. It might be argued, however, that a writer has higher aims than this, that he writes that children may have life more abundantly, seeing through the author's eyes the beauty

97

and wonder and truth of the world around him and the world of the imagination. If this is so, I am not mistaken in thinking that (to consider only a few of her younger contemporaries) there is more rich and enduring delight in the books of William Mayne, Rosemary Sutcliff, Ian Serraillier and Philippa Pearce.

The first urgent need after the war was for new editions of the children's classics and these were slow to come from British houses. An opportunist publisher introduced the American 'Rainbow Classics' and these, although aggressively American in style, stopped the gap reasonably well. In 1949 Dent's Children's Illustrated Classics began to appear in a post-war, but still old-fashioned, format. Individual editions of quality appeared from other publishers. Several notable editions of Andersen were issued, including a reprint of the Rex Whistler edition in 1948, an Oxford Classics edition in 1945, an interestingly unusual book from Peter Lunn in 1947 with illustrations a little 'after' Whistler by Philip Gough, and a lavish picture-book of *The Ugly Duckling* in Penguin's ill-fated Porpoise Books in 1948. The Grimm stories also received interesting treatment from Peter Lunn. Routledge's issued a scholarly complete edition of Grimm in 1948, and Cassells produced a *Travelling Musicians* with magnificent drawings by Hans Fischer. The most impressive Grimm came from Eyre and Spottiswoode in 1946 with powerful, disturbing and creative drawings by Mervyn Peake, perhaps the major achievement of this curious genius.

No other edition of the classics equalled this for creative originality. At the other end of the scale the future was foreshadowed in sinister fashion in a Pitman *Treasure Island* in 1949 "retold in pictures by Peter Jackson".

There were isolated pieces of evidence that children and their reading needs were being considered seriously. An International Youth Book Exhibition at Munich in 1946 was to have permanent results. In 1947 one of the best and most entertaining introductions to children's books, *About Books for Children*, by a distinguished New Zealand librarian, Dorothy Neal White, appeared. In the next year, *Collins Magazine for Boys and Girls*, edited by a writer in the Ransome tradition, Pamela Whitlock, set new and very high standards in periodical publishing, and an equally striking, most influential and somewhat self-consciously well-intended adventure in comics began with the publication in 1950 of *Eagle*. Children who during the war had had limited opportunities for book-buying had to be coaxed back to good habits by the issue of Book Tallies, baby brothers of Book Tokens, which began in 1949.

A phenomenon of post-war publishing was the emergence of the Oxford University Press as a publisher of children's books of the most extraordinary excellence. They had in the past published many individual books of high excellence, but their imprint was associated popularly with 'Rewards' of no particular quality. Now, under the guidance of Geoffrey Cumberlege and with a Children's Editor, Frank Eyre, who had skill in planning and a flair for finding individual books, the 'Reward' trade was thrown overboard. During the next few years, under Eyre and later John Bell, Amen House established a policy of producing a limited number of books each year, each selected for its excellence and originality and each designed in every detail.

(i) *Picture-Books after the War*

In 1948 Penguins introduced a new series of Porpoise Books. These were picture-books of some forty-eight pages, with board covers and jackets, brilliantly printed in colour, and sold at 3s. 6d. The general editor was Grace Hogarth. This was an Anglo-American enterprise and of the first four titles, two were by English artists. Four others were announced, but they never appeared. The series, of the highest quality and the greatest interest, unaccountably failed.

The two English contributors to Porpoise Books were the outstanding author-artists of this age, Edward Ardizzone and V. H. Drummond. Both were well known before 1948 but were then developing their highly individual styles. Ardizzone's Porpoise Book: *Paul, the Hero of the Fire* was not among his best, but in the same year he produced a big picture-book in his finest manner, *Nicholas and the Fast-moving Diesel*, an amusing, highly unconvincing story set in the richly detailed landscape which is the hallmark of his style. In the following year he returned to his 'Tim' books with *Tim to the Rescue*. This, although smaller than the pre-war 'Tims', came up to the highest expectations. Written in an unobtrusively exquisite prose, and drawn with a sure line and fine colour, it was most successfully printed. This was due largely to the artist's method of colour separation which anticipated some of the printer's difficulties.

V. H. Drummond contributed *The Flying Postman* to Porpoise Books. This was a pleasing essay in her manner of serious nonsense. Probably her best book had been published immediately after the war in 1945; *Miss Anna Truly* contained many of her favourite motifs: an idyllic countryside, a charmingly idealised, but recognisable, London in which one might picnic in Albermarle Street, a set of everyday characters in not quite everyday situations, a king who could clown without loss of dignity – this last destined to become a recurrent figure in her work. V. H. Drummond was to write other delightful and characteristic books, including *Lady Talavera* [1946], *The Mountain that Laughed* [1947] and *Tidgie's Innings* [1948], but she added nothing new to *Miss Anna Truly*, which, with its admirable story, quietly excellent writing, and disarmingly naïve drawing, remains one of the minor masterpieces of the English picture-book.

There could hardly be a greater contrast than that between *Miss Anna Truly* and *Captain Slaughterboard*. V. H. Drummond's picture of society is essentially kindly and sane; Mervyn Peake's is vital and exuberant but grotesque and violent in the extreme. *Captain Slaughterboard Drops Anchor* [1945] was an individual achievement of a high order. It delighted some children (and adults) as much as it distressed others. Peake's nightmare visions were something quite new in children's books; he might owe a little technically to Dicky Doyle but his true master was Hieronymus Bosch. His technical virtuosity was achieved by comparatively simple means, and the impression of colour was conveyed economically by the use of tinted papers.

Other picture-books were less sensational. Leslie Wood continued to do good work in the continental manner, in Diana Ross's *Whoo, Whoo, the Wind Blew* and *Callers at Our House* [both 1946]; Jack Townend used simpler means with equal force and humour in *A Story about Ducks* [1946]. Harold Jones used a traditional English style in *The Enchanted Night* [1947]. An interesting and unusual book was *Come In* [1947], with a text by Olive Dehn and pictures by Katherine Gell; this dealt in quiet naturalistic terms with a day in the life of an ordinary family. *The Little Train* [1946] was a story, with pictures by Dorothy Craigie, in the familiar engine-with-human-characteristics manner; its distinction lay in the author of the text, Graham Greene.

Some interesting picture-books came from abroad. The Oxford University Press published in 1948 a brilliant book from Holland, *The Book of the Four Coloured Pencils*, which exploited a simple idea with great force. A Danish book, *Paul Alone in the World* [1948], was a model of balance between word and picture. More books of Virginia Lee Burton came from America, including her most successful, *The Little House* [1947], which had won the Caldecott Medal. An interesting newcomer was Hardie Gramatky, a former member of Disney's team of artists, whose *Little Toot* [1946] showed high humour and great technical virtuosity.

(ii) *Imagination after the War*

If, Chinese-fashion, 1905 was the Year of the Psammead, 1945 was the Year of Miss Price. The publication towards the end of the year of *The Magic Bedknob* – curiously it appeared first in the United States – introduced a new writer of the first rank, Mary Norton. In two years' time *Bonfires and Broomsticks* reinforced the conviction that here was a writer who could without hesitation be set beside the great writers of the past. There were flaws in both books which came from inexperience, but in conception, in style, in humour and in personality they were of the highest excellence.

The central character of *The Magic Bedknob* was Miss Price, a country lady who looked like the secretary of the Women's Institute but who was a witch. Her magic and the magic of the bedknob which the children in the story operate are closely related, and Mary Norton manipulated the supernatural elements in her story, often but not only for comic effect, with almost unfailing skill. The book is extremely funny but the fun is of a serious kind, and in the sequel which goes back in time – the bed had travelled in space – the serious element was more evident. A characteristic of Mary Norton's invention, which became more pronounced in her later books, was the carefully detailed evidence which supported her main thesis. An example of this, in *The Magic Bedknob*, is the exciting episode on the desert island – no longer deserted. In this it is not sufficient that Miss Price turns the witch-doctor into a toad; the reader is shown the whole process in convincing detail.

". . . she held out her two arms toward the witch-doctor as if to ward him off with the broomstick. He stopped, with knees bent, about to jump. Then he seemed to shrink and dwindle. He sank downwards into his legs as if the heat of the fire was melting him. The children held their breaths as they watched. Every part of him was shrinking at the same time. It reminded Carey of what happened to a lead soldier when you threw it on the fire, but instead of a blob of silver, the witch-doctor melted into a minute blob of gold, a tiny yellowish object, barely distinguishable upon the sandy ground".

The Carnegie Medal for 1946 was awarded to Elizabeth Goudge for *The Little White Horse*. This was true fantasy, but of a very different kind from Mary Norton's. Elizabeth Goudge told a story of the endless war of good and evil but dressed it up in so much sweetness and whimsy that the meaning was almost lost. The book was written with great technical competence. The characters, good and bad, had three-dimensional realism; the setting, an idealised Devon, was drawn with equal affection and conviction – it is the most successful element in the book. *The Little White Horse* has been blamed for sentimentality; the criticism is just, but there are so many good things in the book, a beautifully detailed landscape, memorable caricatures, brilliantly contrived episodes, that it is quite possible to forget the fundamental lack of humour. Elizabeth Goudge wrote for children before and after this book, but here was her most successful contribution, a book on which she lavished all the craft of a phenomenally successful novelist.

The excellent illustrations to *The Little White Horse* were by C. Walter Hodges. Into them crept a sense of fun which was lacking in the text. In his own *The Flying House* [1947] Hodges' humour was unrestricted. This was a rare funny book, briskly written and illustrated with a tireless exuberance. There was plenty of exuberance also in Eric Linklater's *The Pirates of the Deep Green Sea* [1949]. This was another of the fantasies which began as a joke and acquired a deeper significance as it went on, but the book was over-long and its strength was dissipated.

In 1947 Rumer Godden, another distinguished writer who turned from success as an adult novelist to write without condescension fine stories for children, published *The Dolls' House*, the first and in some way the best of the books in which she explored the subtleties of doll-psychology. It was a book marked equally by integrity and exquisite writing.

Two collections of masterly short-stories appeared. In 1947 the *Collected Stories for Children* of Walter de la Mare was published. None of the stories was new, but the book gave an opportunity for assessing the achievement of the most gifted writer of the century who had dedicated his finest powers to delighting children. It also provided the opportunity of awarding De la Mare the Carnegie Medal. In 1949 appeared the first book of a writer who had a little of De la Mare's strong and delicate fantasy and his easy mastery of words. Barbara Leonie Picard's *The Mermaid and the Simpleton* was a book of invented fairy tales which showed not only a deep understanding of the roots of the folk-tale but a spiritual kinship with the anonymous makers of fairy tales.

Two interesting fantasies – if the stories in which there are no purely supernatural elements occur can be so called – came from America. *Stuart Little* [1946] by the well-known humorist E. B. White dealt with the unusual second son of Mr. and Mrs. Little, a solid middle-class couple. Stuart was only as big as a mouse; in fact he *was* a mouse. White chose to tell his incredible story in a perfectly matter-of-fact way which emphasised its comic incongruities. *Stuart Little* is a book which inspires affection. *The Twenty-One Balloons* [1950] produces a feeling of bemused admiration. William Pene du Bois, as writer and artist, has always been fascinated by machinery, and in this book, a winner of the Newbery Medal, fantastic humour was married to technical accuracy. The starting-point of the story was the explosion of Krakatoa, which blew that island to dust. This was well-known history, but it was less well-known that Krakatoa had a complex society under a Restaurant Government and a highly mechanised way of life. The absurdities were fully documented in the author's precise blue-print drawings.

The last major fantasy of the immediate post-war years looked back and ahead. *The Lion, the Witch, and the Wardrobe* [1950] was by C. S. Lewis, a most distinguished scholar and theologian who turned to the children's fantasy as a suitable vehicle for his philosophical and theological ideas. The first chronicle of the holy land of Narnia had something of the magical mysticism of George Macdonald with E. Nesbit's colloquial humour. It was derivative only in the sense that all great literature belongs to a tradition. *The Lion, the Witch, and the Wardrobe* was a major event of 1950; for the full appreciation of Lewis's conception and achievement one had to wait six years until the final chapter in the history of Narnia had been written.

The publication of *The Weaver Birds* in 1944 passed almost unnoticed. There was nothing unusual about slim volumes by young poets, particularly in wartime. *The Weaver Birds* was the first book of the first poet since De la Mare and Eleanor Farjeon to speak the authentic language of childhood. In 1946 the Oxford University Press published a selection of these poems, with others, in a volume designed most exquisitely for children under the title *Thomas and the Sparrow*. The arrival of Ian Serraillier was as exciting in its way as the arrival of Mary Norton; both were writers of original genius, both were to prove the least prolific of writers. *Thomas and the Sparrow*, for which the Belgian artist Mark Severin provided illustrations which extended the range of the poems, was remarkable for the verbal and rhythmic virtuosity of the verse and for the exuberance of the imagery.

Another new poet, James Reeves, showed a more conventional talent in *The Wandering Moon* [1946]. These verses, written in one sustained effort, had considerable charm and wit, an original imagination and technical ingenuity.

Eleanor Farjeon's *The Starry Floor* [1949] was another of her groups of linked poems which covered a wide range of moods and included some of her most profound ideas. In 1950 her most familiar poem, *Mrs. Malone*, reappeared in a charming miniature volume. Her old friend Walter de la Mare had no new poems for children, but *Peacock Pie* made a fresh appearance with wonderfully wise and penetrating drawings by Ardizzone. No anthologies of the first interest were published. Two books edited and decorated by M. C. Green – *Stars and Primroses* [1945] and *Magic Lanterns* [1949] had charm.

(iii) *Adventure after Ransome*

Arthur Ransome brought to an end his stories of the 'Swallows and Amazons' in 1947 with *Great Northern?* The stories, twelve in number, had taken seventeen years in the telling and the original Swallows and Amazons had long since grown up. *Great Northern?* closed the series in magnificent style. This was a book containing all Ransome's favourite themes and ideas; it was full of practical details, sailing and birds were at the heart of it, and at the core of its plot was a problem of responsibility. Once again, as in *Pigeon Post*, the key character was Dick, the clever boy, who was Ransome's most interesting invention. Looking back from *Great Northern?* it was possible to see Ransome's achievement as a whole, with its organic growth. Fine story-telling, unerring characterisation, faithful concern for detail, all had contributed to Ransome's success; but above all the books were seen to embody a point of view, a philosophy almost, firmly held and consistently developed through twelve incomparable volumes.

Great Northern? dwarfed the other adventure stories of the post-war years. Many showed the Ransome influence in subject or treatment like Garry Hogg's *Sealed Orders* [1948], a story of what is now called an initiative test, Pamela Hill's charming story of sailing in Chichester Harbour, *Wind and Weather Permitting* [1946], C. E. Roberts' stories of 'Pikey's Steep', Eleanor Graham's *Head o' Mey* [1947] and, perhaps the most successfully derivative, Olivia Fitzroy's stories of Scottish adventures (but her social values were less sound than Ransome's).

Several writers used Ransome as a starting point for stories in their own manner. Peter Dawlish started his 'Dauntless' stories in 1947 with *Dauntless Finds Her Crew;* Ransome had been a skilled amateur sailor, Dawlish was a professional, and there is a difference in the development of their story which reflects this difference in attitude. Dawlish's writing lacked distinction, but he was an honest observer and an expert in his own field, as his 'Career Book' *The First Tripper* [1947] clearly showed. Another good observer started modestly in 1947; this was Monica Edwards whose *Wish for a Pony*, almost a conventional pony-book, showed little promise of the wisdom and integrity to come. Stephen Fennimore, in *Bush Holiday* [1948] and *Bush Voyage* [1950], offered somewhat Ransome-like qualities of character in an Australian setting. Geoffrey Trease boldly challenged comparisons by choosing Ransome's Lakeland as a setting of *No Boats on Bannermere* [1949], the first of an interesting series showing the social, educational and sexual maturing of a group of attractive young people. The weakest part of his invention was in plot which was both conventional and unconvincing.

A year earlier Elfrida Vipont published a book which, while attempting no such thing, pushed outwards the boundaries of the school story. *The Lark in the Morn* must be considered with its sequel *The Lark on the Wing* [1950], which won the Carnegie Medal. These two radiant books told the story of a girl, Kit Haverard, from early schooldays to the brink of a career and of marriage. It has always been Elfrida Vipont's characteristic that she sees life whole, and the fun, the frustration, the grief and the wisdom of these two books were all part of an overall view of life. Pervading the books was a rich sense of the power of goodness. In the short view the 'Lark' books lacked distinction of style; their merits were not literary, but they were so firmly based in understanding and faith that they rose far above the level to which they superficially belonged. The Quaker and musical backgrounds were most beautifully sustained.

Some writers managed to inject new life into the worn-out traditional cliché-stories. Ian Serraillier told a fundamentally improbable yarn with great exuberance and style in *They Raced for Treasure* [1946]. Even the school-story was capable of revitalising. The veteran writer of school-stories, Gunby Hadath, far surpassed his previous best in *The March of Time* [1946], an interesting study of a public school in war-time. In *Princess Gwyn*, Olive C. Dougan proved that it was possible to write a girls' school story with individual characters and sensible values, and in *Nancy Finds Herself* [1947] and *The Forbidden Holiday* [1948] demonstrated that she could do it again. By far the best of the girls' school-stories was *Autumn Term* [1948] in which Antonia Forest used the conventional materials as if they had come freshly to hand. A. Stephen Tring [Laurence Meynell] brought his considerable technical ability to the boys' story in *The Old Gang* [1947] and in *Penny*

Dreadful [1949] created a girl counterpart to 'William' who had better values, more reality and, it must be confessed, less vitality than Richmal Crompton's original.

Two of the earliest Carnegie Medal-winners were still writing. Eve Garnett, over a decade after *The Family from One End Street*, published her next book *In and Out and Roundabout* [1948], a set of short stories set in and about the Ruggles' little town and bearing the same signs of honest, affectionate, unsentimental observation of poor people. Noel Streatfeild produced a competent book in *Party Frock* [1946] and a fine one in *The Painted Garden* [1949] which, in her best manner, explored the fabulous world of Hollywood and the motives of her characters with equal skill.

Martha Robinson was a far less skilled writer, but her *A House of Their Own* [1949] was notable as a serious, and reasonably successful, study of the effects of the current housing shortage on a typical family. Here at least was a book written not in a vacuum but in a world beset with difficulties. Cecil Day Lewis's *The Otterbury Incident* [1948], too, was contemporary. Lewis based his story on the French film *Nous Les Gosses* and matched the film's wit and speed with appropriate words. A writer who, without using an obviously contemporary setting was clearly modern in her approach to her story and her characters was Margaret Lovett, a most interesting writer who failed to maintain her original promise. *Adventure for Fivepence* [1945] and *Family Pie* [1947] showed a most mature understanding of behaviour and mastery of dialogue. She was particularly successful in the portrayal of natural and satisfying family relationships.

Margaret Lovett's were quiet stories. Kathleen Wallace's were almost silent. *The Gentle Shadows* [1947], a ghost story, and *Cross the Bridge and See* [1949], a story of the Chinese way of life, were subtly conceived and beautifully written but so delicate in their inferences that they evaded all but the most sensitive of young readers. *Embroidery Mary* [1948] was quiet, but P. M. Warner understood her readers as well as her characters and this charming story, with its accurate material, has not lacked readers.

John Lehmann was one of the publishers who, like Blackwell in the 'twenties, looked for young writers to bring their adult talents to the rescue of children's books. He was only partially successful, possibly because his experiment was short-lived. The best book from his house was *Savage Gold* [1946], a fine story of Africa by the poet Roy Fuller which was exciting enough for any boy but which had mature qualities of style and observation. Roy Fuller's later attempt to write a boy's detective-story – *With My Little Eye* [1948] – was over-sophisticated, and a third Lehmann book – P. H. Newby's *Spirit of Jem* [1947] was so clever as to be almost unreadable. Less experimental publishers also turned to established adult writers for children's books. Norman Collins' *Black Ivory* [1948] was the first-fruit of *Collins' Magazine*, in which it appeared as the first serial. It was a strong, clever story of the Slave Trade, which not even Collins' brilliant writing could make very palatable. This was professional fiction-writing, highly competent, without true conviction. Two adventure stories by little-known writers outclassed him for authenticity – A. S. Kennard-Davis' *A Farm in Cedar Valley* [1948] was a beautifully simple and convincing story of first hand experience in Kenya; Edward Fenton's *Aleko's Island* [1947] was a moving, subtle, poetical investigation of a Greek boy's mind and thought. Too remote to be widely successful, it has been for a few children a major landmark in the appreciation of literature.

Richard Armstrong, whose sequel to *The Mystery of Obadiah*, *Sabotage at the Forge*, had appeared in 1946, won the Carnegie Medal in 1948 with *Sea Change*. It is interesting to compare this with Peter Dawlish's *First Tripper*. Dawlish's was a competent 'Career Book', providing information about the Merchant Service within the framework of an interesting story. *Sea Change* was also about the Merchant Navy. It was equally informative and authentic, for both writers were writing out of their own experience. As a story *Sea Change* has no great advantage of *First Tripper*. Armstrong, however, had brought back from sea not only a rich store of experience but also a philosophy. He believed passionately in the virtue of hard work, and that was the real theme of *Sea Change*. It was a very fine story, written with unobtrusive excellence and conveying its lessons in an acceptable way. Armstrong was to write many more books on the same theme, but in *Sea Change* he balanced most successfully the elements of purpose and entertainment in which an adventure story became a manifesto on the dignity of labour.

Science fiction, lacking in distinction since Donald Suddaby's *Lost Men in the Grass*, achieved literary status again with David Craigie's *The Voyage of Luna I* [1948]. This story of a boy's flight to the Moon was of no more than average interest as science; the vivid writing gave it a quality of its own. Fine writing, also, combined with psychological insight, lifted *There's No Escape* right out of the international thriller-class to which it superficially belonged; Ian Serraillier's story had pace and suspense, but it had above all style. David Severn escaped from his own success as a writer of Ransomish open-air series with *Dream Gold* [1949], a brilliantly contrived adventure story on a 'Time' theme. In *They Found a Cave* [1949] English children were introduced to a new writer from the Antipodes whose story of adventures in Tasmania was full of high promise. This promise Nan Chauncy was to redeem in full in the next ten years.

The immediate post-war years were Geoffrey Trease's best as an historical novelist. His *Trumpets in the West* found plenty of action and excitement in the Monmouth Rebellion but showed the military operations against the life of the times with the accompaniment of Purcell's music. *The Hills of Varna* [1948] represented perhaps the highest reach of his achievement. This was a story of the Renaissance concerned with the fate of a classical manuscript. This, too, was a story of action growing naturally from the circumstances of the time and the personalities of the principal character. Trease was particularly successful in bringing out the incongruous elements of culture and barbarism in Renaissance Europe.

A book by Ivy Bolton, *Son of the Land* [1948], was a sharp social comment on the Peasants' Revolt much in Trease's own manner. Joan Selby-Lowndes' two stories of Reformation England were less forceful but quietly convincing. *Royal Chase* [1947] and *Tudor Star* [1949] showed some of the effects of the Dissolution of the Monasteries on a small country community. There was not much historical message in Primrose Cumming's *The Great Horses* [1946]; this was an admirable idea – the story of three horses from the Norman Conquest to the present day – carried out with a little less than excellence.

A major historical novelist made her appearance in 1949. Cynthia Harnett had been well-known before the war for lovely picture-books of country life written and drawn in collaboration with her cousin Vernon Stokes. *The Great House* [1949] was a very quiet, almost static, story about an architect practising the new style in the days of William and Mary. The invention in *The Great House* was weak, but what gave the book its distinction was the multitude of minute and authentic details of which it was made. This was the work of a scholar and – as the illustrations showed – an artist.

(ix) *Pursuit of Knowledge*

The major post-war achievement in informative literature was unquestionably the *Oxford Junior Encyclopaedia*, the first of whose twelve volumes appeared in 1948. This was the first serious attempt to provide children with an encyclopaedia designed on the same principles as the great encyclopaedias for adults. The material was arranged not in isolated scraps of information but in full-scale articles. As the work was published in volumes over a long period, each volume was self-contained (although there were necessarily cross-references). This had the advantage of emphasising the interrelation of subjects. It could not be said that the *Oxford Junior Encyclopaedia* was entirely successful. It did not solve all the problems latent in its form, nor did all the contributors reconcile simplicity with authenticity. It was not always clear for whom the work was intended. It nevertheless gave its readers credit for intelligence and interest; it never condescended.

This was the beginning of the great age of non-fictional series. There had been many series before, some of them – like the Oxford 'Pageant of Progress' – of the highest excellence. After the War, publishers, more sensitive than ever before to public opinion, and particularly the opinion of teachers and librarians, found in series the answer to many of their problems. If one book in a series was satisfactory, the others would sell to schools and libraries on the reputation of the first. Some of the series were the work of a single writer like Agnes Allen, whose 'stories' began in 1947 with *The Story of the Village*. These studies in social history were competently written, if a little dull, and reasonably well documented. The illustrations, by Jack Allen, were closely integrated with the text.

A typical series was the Phoenix House 'Excursions', of which Andrew Buchanan's *Going to the Cinema* [1941] was a good example. Excursion Books were useful and lively guides to the enjoyment of the arts of living; like most series this went on after the initial impetus had been lost. The Oxford 'New Playbooks of Science' were issued sparingly and the initial high standard was well maintained. Herbert McKay's *Tricks of light and colour* [1947] was a good example with its brisk style and practical approach.

The series technique lends itself most successfully to the treatment of biography; the material is unlikely to run out and there is fair scope for the author's individuality. Fabers introduced an admirable series of biographical studies after the war, of which Russell Grenfell's *Nelson the Sailor* [1949] was typical. These were original in approach and simple in selection of material rather than in expression; they were at least as much books for adults. Methuen's 'Story Biographies' had the physical format of children's books; they were not less original in treatment.

One of them, Geoffrey Trease's *Fortune My Foe* [1949] attempted to explain to children the complex character and career of Sir Walter Raleigh, without perhaps succeeding in reconciling the philosopher and the pirate in his subject. The S.C.M. 'Torch Biographies' had considerably less literary distinction, but despite colourless writing and inadequate format these lives of men and women who were great in spirit had real value. In *Despite the Colour Bar* [1946] A. M. Pullen told the story of George Washington Carver, and other volumes dealt with Smuts, Thring of Uppingham and Dr. Aggrey.

It was still possible for the non-fictional book out of series to make its way, like Malcolm Saville's pleasant *Jane's Country Year* [1946] which provides a simple and persuasively written guide to the countryside; G. D. Fisher's *Hut Country Days* [1948] had less ease of style but more authority. C. H. Abrahall's *Prelude* [1947] was a remarkable, beautifully designed, story of the childhood of Eileen Joyce the pianist. The treatment was so free as to border on the fictional, but the lively and sensitive writing was irresistable. The most interesting treatment of informative material was in *The Map that Came to Life* [1948] in which H. J. Deverson, with exceedingly clever drawings by R. Lampitt, expounded the technique of map-reading in picture-book form, much as the early Puffin Picture Books had done.

CHAPTER 8

WIDENING HORIZONS

THE 'fifties are too close for a confident assessment of their achievements to be made; the most that can safely be done is a brief glance at the main trends and the principal writers. One thing is clear: the general standard, literary and physical, has been high in the past ten years. Authors and publishers have taken children's books seriously; possibly a little too seriously. The earnestness, the purposeful professionalism of the 'fifties produced books for which teachers and librarians ask; it was less likely to produce the book of individual genius. Such books, however, have a habit of breaking through; the 'fifties have seen the arrival of *The Borrowers*, of William Mayne and Philippa Pearce, of Rosemary Sutcliff.

Books, which had survived the threat of cinema and radio, faced an apparent adversary in television, which turned out after all to be a friend. If many of the so-called children's programmes had little to commend them as entertainment or education, some were excellent, using new material or turning to the great stories of the past and adapting them with unexpected consideration. More important, television stimulated an interest in many subjects, such as ballet and archeology, which had previously been the concern of a small minority, and children turned to books for further enlightenment. Faced with a new demand, publishers issued many more books, most of them inevitably in series, of an informative kind.

Professional concern with children's reading increased greatly. The Ministry of Education had issued a directive to schools to improve their libraries, and the teacher-librarian appeared for the first time as an important factor in the economics of book-production. A huge new market opened to the publisher. Meanwhile the public library service to children developed, if unevenly. A major weakness in the children's library had always been the lack of organised training for children's librarians. In 1951 the Youth Libraries Section of the Library Association arranged a week-end school, the first of a continuing series, at Tring, where training was one of the principal subjects discussed. Partly as a result of this, the first full-time course was held for six weeks, at the North-Western Polytechnic, London, in 1954. This became a bi-annual event; admittedly not the solution to the problem of training, it was the first tentative step towards a solution. In 1958 a new qualification, the Teacher-librarian Certificate, was inaugurated by a joint board of the Library Association and the School Library Association.

In 1953 the American Library Association had published *The Unreluctant Years* by Lilian H. Smith. This introduction to the art of selecting books for children, by the former head of Boys' and Girls' Book House in Toronto, became necessary reading for all who felt any concern for the books which children read. Another indication of increasing interest in children's books was the institution of the Hans Christian Andersen Medal, to be awarded in alternate years to a distinguished children's author. This award, by the International Board on Books for Young People, enjoys an international reputation; but, as Eileen Colwell pointed out in an article in *Junior Bookshelf* [July, 1958], the task of comparing books in a multitude of different languages is "impossible". Lesser, but still considerable, difficulties faced the Library Association in making a new award for illustration, the Kate Greenaway Medal, which was instituted in 1955 but not awarded until the following year. The Committee selecting a suitable book for this award have been unable to make comparisons between illustrations of many different kinds, in many different media, and with many different purposes, and have limited their choice, in effect, to a picture-book.

Evidence of a general increase in interest in children's books and their writers was provided by such events as the appointment of Arthur Ransome as a C.B.E. in 1952 (in the same year he received an honorary doctorate from Leeds) and the publication in the *Sunday Times* during 1958 of a list of one hundred best books, an undertaking which aroused wide public interest and controversy.

With the ending of wartime restrictions on materials and labour, books multiplied alarmingly. The vast annual output of British publishers became a matter of real anxiety to everyone concerned either as distributors or purchasers. It was increasingly difficult to keep track of worth-while books, and the existing reviewing journals became quite inadequate. The national daily and Sunday newspapers, and the literary weeklies, continued to regard children's books as of seasonal interest, although a little more space was allowed for reviewing (and advertising) them. *The Times Literary Supplement*, while still clinging to the belief that children's books belonged to Spring and Christmas, gave up two long supplements a year to an extended critical consideration of them. Among specialist journals, the *School Librarian* expanded its reviews considerably, and the *Journal of Education* published vigorous and controversial articles on many aspects of children's books and reading. The best of these were later collected under the editorship of Boris Ford as *Young Writers, Young Readers* [1960].

A phenomenon of post-war publishing was the vast increase in paper-backed books. These were the result of changed habits of reading and in turn they fostered the change. A few publishers followed the lead of Penguin Books in producing paper-backs especially for children, but it was not these so much as those produced for the adult market which a new generation of young readers made their own. They took over, much as they had taken over *Robinson Crusoe* and *Gulliver's Travels*, many of the books designed for their elders and now readily accessible to them at home or on the book-stalls; in particular the stories of war, prison-camps and atrocities became food for young stomachs ill prepared for such strong meat.

In the 'fifties the 'C stream' came into its own. Publishers became acutely aware of the need for books for the reluctant reader, and commissioned many books for them. Some of these, simple in vocabulary and syntax but dealing with suitably unchildish themes, were excellently done; most were all too clearly 'purpose-made'. There was a great, and unfilled, need for writers who could write naturally and unselfconsciously within the range of the slow reader.

(i) *Picture-books*

American picture-books, which in the 'thirties had provided so valuable a stimulus to British artists, in the 'fifties threatened to swamp the market. When the Kate Greenaway Medal was instituted, it proved impossible to make a satisfactory award in the first and third years; it is difficult to believe that this was due to a lack of local talent. A visit to any bookshop showed that there was no dearth of books, but ever since the arrival of the Little Golden Books in 1950, combining good colour-printing and low cost, it was difficult for a British publisher to compete unless he was assured of large overseas sales.

This is not to complain of all the imports. Any country would be the better for Ludwig Bemelman's *Madeline* [1952] or Roger Duvoisin's *Petunia* [1958]. Many of the continental books, too, now being issued in English editions were immensely stimulating. Very fine line and colour distinguished the work of Alois Carigiet [*A Bell for Ursli*, 1950], Felix Hoffmann [*The Wolf and the Seven Little Kids*, 1958], and Reiner

Zimnik [*Jonah the Fisherman*, 1957], and there were others not far short of this standard. It was perhaps not entirely surprising that few new British picture-book artists appeared, and only one, Gerald Rose, was of the first rank. Rose's *How St. Francis Tamed the Wolf* [1958] to a text by his wife Elizabeth showed high spirits and a sense of colour which was almost continental in its freedom from inhibition.

The best British work was by artists of long established repute. Helen Binyon brought a fine restraint and sense of form to *An Everyday Alphabet* [1952] which showed children at their everyday activities; an important book because of its very simplicity. Harold Jones, whose work in the years since *This Year, Next Year* had been unremarkable, surprised his admirers with the wealth and variety of *Lavender's Blue*, a book of nursery rhymes edited by Kathleen Lines. This was a picture-book in the true English tradition, well-drawn, humorous, lively yet mannered. The desire of the Library Association to honour work of this kind led directly to the institution of the Kate Greenaway Medal.

There was no such surprise in Edward Ardizzone's work, only a deep satisfaction that drawing should be so true and kindly. The post-war 'Little Tim' books showed none of the weakened inspiration common in sequels, only an increased certainty of draughtsmanship and a richer appreciation of people. *Tim and Charlotte* [1951], *Tim in Danger* [1953] and *Tim All Alone* [1956] were beautifully drawn and printed and told in a deceptively simple prose.

Tim All Alone was honoured with the first Kate Greenaway Medal. Two years later the Medal went to V. H. Drummond for another sequel, *Mrs. Easter and the Storks* [1957]. This, too, was a picture-book in which prose style played as important a part as draughtsmanship. Exuberantly coloured, full of a sense of fun and of absurdity, this was a book which belonged, like Ardizzone's and Jones's, to the English tradition. The third Kate Greenaway Medal was awarded to William Stobbs for remarkable illustrations to *Kashtanka* [1959], a charming, unfamiliar story by Chekov. Stobbs was an artist of wide versatility who, during the 'fifties (his work was little-known before), was in great demand as an illustrator of adventure stories and historical romances. His work in *Kashtanka* used Russian motifs with equal vigour and charm, and showed a gentle humour equal to Chekov's own. *Kashtanka* was a story with pictures rather than a picture-book, but there was clear evidence in it that Stobbs was potentially a maker of picture-books in the great English tradition.

(ii) *Beyond Realism*

Many writers have been ready to speak against the prevailing materialism of the post-war world, none more consistently than C. S. Lewis. Lewis, a most distinguished scholar and theologian who had enjoyed in childhood the stories of George Macdonald and E. Nesbit, turned to the allegorical fantasy as the most suitable vehicle for some of his philosophical and moral ideas. In seven stories he traced the history of the land of Narnia from its creation by the great lion Aslan to its final destruction in a grand apocalyptic conclusion. In some of the stories, particularly the earlier part of *The Magician's Nephew* [1955], the influence of E. Nesbit was strong. In all of them, there was an uneasy mixture of styles, with schoolboy slang and 'lofty' rhetoric in incongruous juxtaposition. As narrative and as allegory they were most brilliantly successful. Lewis had a great gift for telling a tale. The swift action, the detailed setting, and the many memorable characters, comical and serious, contributed to stories which were exciting, convincing and highly readable. It was quite possible to read the 'Narnia' stories as fine tales of action. They are also expositions of Lewis's ideas of the endless struggle between good and evil.

C. S. Lewis's books were great in conception, rather less than great in execution. The grandeur of the central theme was marred by occasional trivialities of expression and by a fundamental improbability; it was always difficult to accept the translation of the schoolboy Peter into the High King Peter of Narnia. No such reservations apply to *The Borrowers*. Of the decade's fantasies this alone was completely harmonious. Children have always loved worlds in miniature; they stole Swift's biting satire and turned it into an imaginative frolic, just as, more recently, they found delight in T. H. White's finely melancholy fantasy *Mistress Masham's Repose* [1947]. Mary Norton owed a little to the tradition of Lilliput but more to her own minute close-up view of life. The Borrowers, tiny creatures whose home is under the floor and behind the skirting and who live by borrowing from humans, were drawn from the life. The precise definition of every detail of the story, as exact as an architect's scale drawing, gave to Mary Norton's imaginings an inescapable conviction. Not for her the easy framework of a dream. Her Borrowers are real little people fighting a desperate rear-guard action against a society in which they can have little place. Only a tiny ray of hope makes the stories (for two sequels have followed the fortunes of the Borrowers across the fields and down the stream) bearable. It is in fact arguable that this is not fantasy. There is no magic.

The reader makes one concession to probability, in accepting the existence of such tiny creatures; after this everything is worked out in strictly naturalistic terms.

The Borrowers by its idea alone, one of the few really original ideas in children's literature, would have been a landmark. In the working out of detail, in the creation not only of character but of a whole society, and above all in the exquisite writing, the idea turned into a flawless book. Mary Norton's prose is a model to study; it is clean and strong, free from affectation and with only enough mannerism to give it personality. It is the perfect vehicle for this marvellous story of Pod, Homily and Arrietty and of the lovely home they made under the floor-boards.

Mary Norton and C. S. Lewis dominated the 'fifties so effectively that it is difficult to do justice to lesser writers of fantasy. Not since the 'thirties had imagination been so strong and wide-ranging. Naomi Mitchison, a writer who so often came almost within grasping distance of greatness, produced in 1950 *The Big House*, a fine story of the past and present in Scotland, full of characteristic social comment. This had passages of a haunting beauty and melancholy, but its varying elements were imperfectly reconciled. Richard Armstrong's *Wanderlust* [1952] was nearly a classical fantasy of the De la Mare kind. This story of a little monkey's voyages embodied an allegory of man's endless quest; it was an important theme, in which the author believed passionately but the style failed to rise to the greatness of the occasion. Another book which attempted a great heroic theme was Helen Clare's *Merlin's Magic* [1953], and here, too, the writer was not up to her theme. There were heroic undertones, too, in Roger Lancelyn Green's *The Land of the Lord High Tiger* [1958], a fantasy of the school of Tolkien and Lewis; Green was a scholar who had made the early imaginative literature of children his own province, and his story was inevitably pastiche, though of a most delightful kind.

Other fantasies had less lofty aims, and were in consequence more immediately successful. In *The Children of Green Knowe* [1954] Lucy M. Boston showed the meeting of past and present in her ancient Midland home. This sad, beautiful story, essentially poetical in conception, was rather too elusive to find a wide audience; for individual children it became a most memorable and formative experience.

It was a good period for humorous writing. Some writers, like Ada Harrison in *The Doubling Rod* [1957] and the American Edward Eager in *Half Magic* [1954] derived inspiration directly from E. Nesbit. Leila

Berg in *The Adventures of Chunky* [1950] was completely original; not
even J. B. S. Haldane had been more successfully scientific. *Chunky* was
a really funny idea worked out without hesitation. The humour of
The Enormous Apple Pie [1951] was less boisterous. Diana Ross's stories
of Miss Pussy and her foil, the wicked Jackanapes, were gentle, sincere
and beautifully written. In *The People in the Garden* [1954], Lorna Wood
began a series of lively, genuinely funny stories about magic; sharp
characterisation lent conviction to her witches and her children alike.
Barbara Sleigh's *Carbonel* created a new character, a magical cat, who
promised to possess the kind of immortality which had belonged to
Worzel Gummidge.

Some of the best fantasies came from the Continent, like Marcel
Aymé's *The Wonderful Farm* [1952]. The first of Tove Jansson's
'Moomin' stories reached England in 1950. This was *Finn Family
Moomintroll*, a picture of a wonderfully integrated society, beautifully
realised in prose and in the author's illustrations. It was difficult not to
believe unreservedly in the Moomins and to be moved, to tears and
laughter, by their changing fortunes. There were no tears in *Pippi
Longstocking* [1954], a brilliant realisation of childhood's wish-fantasies
by Astrid Lindgren. Pippi, a loud, herculean, kindly girl who does
what she likes, was horribly convincing. From Germany came a very
charming fantasy, Margot Benary's *The Wicked Enchantment* [1956],
superbly written, dramatic, with a beautifully realised setting in a
mediaeval German town.

No new collections of fairy tales of the first interest were published
in the 'fifties; there was, however, no shortage of books of a somewhat
lower standard. Among isolated examples, *The Golden Phoenix* [1958],
a selection of French-Canadian tales from Marius Barbeau's collection,
was the most interesting. Several publishers, including Muller,
embarked on large-scale series of national folk-tales; the most important of these was the Oxford Myths and Legends, of which the
first volume, James Reeves' *English Fables and Fairy Stories*, was issued
in 1954. Physically these books were of the highest excellence, with
exquisite and appropriate decorations by Joan Kiddell-Monroe. The
quality of the versions was most uneven, however, and the inclusion
in the same volume of the folk-tales, epic stories and mediaeval romances proved not wholly satisfactory.

Many writers continued to use the fairy-tale form for their own
original stories. Of these, the closest in spirit to the folk-tale was
Barbara Leonie Picard who, in spite of the essentially literary quality

of her writing, seemed able to share the thoughts of the primitive anonymous story-tellers of the remote past. The stories in *The Faun and the Woodcutter's Daughter* [1951] were free of the fundamental sophistication to be found in James Reeves and Diana Ross. Reeves' *Pigeons and Princesses* [1956] was charmingly written, and Diana Ross's *The Bridal Gown* [1952] covered a wide range of moods; both, for all their many excellences, were stories written for children, not, as were the real folk-tales, for the satisfaction of the teller.

There was never any doubt about Eleanor Farjeon's inspiration; she wrote because she must. One of the greatest delights of the 'fifties was the success of this veteran writer, who had first delighted children during the First World War and who in her seventies gained the homage of a new generation of readers. For this much credit was due to the Oxford University Press who reissued some of her earlier books and published new ones in most beautiful form. In 1955 *The Little Bookroom* gathered together some of the stories which she had written during a long life; for them Ardizzone provided miraculously fitting illustrations. *The Little Bookroom* won the Carnegie Medal and also the first Hans Christian Andersen Medal. The latter award was particularly appropriate, for Eleanor Farjeon belonged to the Andersen tradition. The exquisite and lovely writing, the pervading humour, the wisdom, the casually fine narrative, all these were characteristics common to both writers.

(iii) *The Age of the Sputnik*

It was to be expected that the decade of the sputnik would see a revival of science-fiction. Not that writers since Jules Verne had ever ceased to find material for adventure stories in deep space. In the 'fifties, however, the rules had been tightened. Every schoolboy knew too much about the theory of space travel; the writer could not indulge his fancy freely.

Most of the science-fiction stories of the 'fifties were of no literary interest. They were in fact the old 'Reward' adventure-stories written according to a slightly modified formula and coloured with pseudo-scientific jargon. A few writers saw in science-fiction the opportunity for genuinely creative writing. Of these the most talented was Donald Suddaby who had, as long ago as 1940, written the terrifying *Lost Men in the Grass*. He wrote only one story about space travel, *The Star Raiders* [1950], in which the technical problems were insufficiently considered, but which was distinguished by a poet's view of the

Venusian landscape. Suddaby was more successful in the ruthless application of a scientific premise, as in *The Death of Metal* [1952], a powerful and convincing story which showed the results of the sudden disintegration of all metals. Like Wells, Suddaby made his story credible by showing the impact of a scientific disaster on a group of very ordinary people. David Severn, who had escaped from his own reputation as a writer in the Ransome tradition in two brilliant books of unexplained magic – *Dream Magic* [1949] and *Drumbeats* [1953] – attempted an essay in formal science fiction in *The Future Took Us* [1958]. There was no great originality in this vision of the future, but the extreme competence of the writing lent conviction to a conventional story. David Craigie was a writer of more originality. In *The Voyage of Luna I* [1948] and still more in *Dark Atlantis* [1952] he showed imaginative powers of a high order. Comparable skill made the huge improbabilities of Bruce Carter's *The Perilous Descent* [1952] acceptable.

These were books on the fringe of science-fiction. Two writers brought original quality to the conventions of space-fiction. Paul Capon was a writer of adult stories in this genre; in *Phobus the Robot Planet* [1955] he told a story for children which was imaginative, lively and extremely competent. Hugh Walters published in 1957 the first of a series of stories about flights to the moon which were distinguished by scientific integrity. *Blast Off at Woomera* [1957] and its successors were the most convincing of space-adventures, because the author, without an excess of scientific jargon, showed the complexity of the problem and the psychological adjustment necessary to a solution. Walters had none of Suddaby's poetry or Craigie's vision. He had instead technical knowledge and an understanding of human behaviour.

(iv) *Novels for Children*

William Mayne's debut in 1953 with *Follow the Footprints* passed almost unnoticed. Although this story contained in embryo all the elements of his later books, and although the plot was most characteristic, it lacked a vital spark. The same was true of his second book. With *A Swarm in May* [1955] it became apparent that a major novelist had arrived. *A Swarm in May* was, of all outmoded things, a boarding-school story, but there had never been a school-story quite like this. The setting was a cathedral choir-school, with its long history and ancient traditions. The hero was a very small boy but the story concerned the whole school, including the staff. It was a picture of a complex and fascinating society. The story was one of hidden treasure –

another outworn theme – and the working-out entirely original and unexpected. Mayne's book, like all his subsequent books, was whole and indivisible; plot, setting, characters, writing, all contributed to the final effect; but the writing was the catalyst. Mayne's prose was a delicate, sensitive instrument, exactly suited to its purpose. The dialogue was exquisitely right, the description (which was never extraneous but always dedicated to forwarding the narrative) was spare and beautiful. Mayne's prose never slipped into poetry, but his eye was that of the poet; he saw the commonplaces of the world around him with the poet's (or the child's) clarity and freshness. Critics who begrudge a child the best in anything have claimed that Mayne is an adult novelist *manqué*. Certainly any of his books is worth the attention of the most exacting adult reader, but in the fine simplicity of his vision as much as in his profound understanding of the minds and instinct of children, he is essentially a children's writer.

Mayne is a prolific writer, and books followed at intervals of less than a year. Although the theme of a search for treasure was recurrent, each story was strikingly original. The scene ranged wide, from Canterbury Cathedral to Sedgemoor, from the Pennines to the Wiltshire Downs. Places are important to Mayne. His stories grow inevitably out of their settings and their characters. He has a fine ear for dialect, and skill in reproducing it in acceptable form. He has become increasingly successful in portraying human relationships, whether simple – in the family atmosphere of *The Member for the Marsh* – or complex – in the situation between Patty and her step-mother in *Underground Alley*. In spite of his love of ancient traditions, he is essentially a contemporary writer. He belongs to the post-war world and understands the social phenomena which have developed since 1945. Understanding and a deep unsentimental affection for young people enrich his wise, subtle stories.

William Mayne received the Carnegie Medal for *A Grass Rope* [1957]. In the following year the same honour went to Philippa Pearce for *Tom's Midnight Garden*. Her first book had competed with *A Swarm in May* as the most exciting experience of 1955. Philippa Pearce is, like Mayne, a highly intelligent young writer. She is the master of a fine sensitive style. She has imagination and a gift for recapturing the emotions and sensations of childhood. *Minnow on the Say* was a little burdened by its plot, but in atmosphere and in freshness it was the most promising first novel of a children's writer for many years. *Tom's Midnight Garden* fully redeemed this promise. This was a fully mature

work, with an original theme developed in a masterly fashion, most understanding treatment of adult and child characters, present and past (for this was a kind of ghost-story), and a hauntingly beautiful evocation of atmosphere. Phillipa Pearce has not hastened to produce a third book, and wisely, for the standard she has set is extremely high. She clearly has much more to say.

The veteran children's novelists have continued to write. Noel Streatfeild, always highly competent, careful in detail, understanding her child characters, has never surpassed her earliest work. Elfrida Vipont has continued into the next generation the chronicles of the Quaker families started with her 'Lark' books; *The Spring of the Year* [1957] and *Flowering Spring* [1960] both had their share of her wisdom, kindliness and profound belief in goodness. Patricia Lynch has in her best work left behind the leprechauns and legends of old Ireland in favour of portraits of lovable, often feckless, very real Irish people. In *Delia Daly of Galloping Green* [1953] and *The Old Black Sea Chest* [1958] she was particularly happy in portraying a satisfactory if uncon-

ventional home life. Naomi Mitchison offered in more narrowly
naturalistic terms a comparable picture of a remote Scottish community in *The Far Harbour* [1957].

Apart from William Mayne and Philippa Pearce the 'fifties have
produced few new writers of unquestionable quality. The Irish writer
Eilis Dillon has written beautifully, notably in *The House on the Shore*
[1955] and *The Singing Cave* [1959], and hovers rather disconcertingly
on the edge of the Celtic twilight. Viola Bayley failed to maintain the
brilliant promise of her Buchanish first story, *The Dark Lantern* [1951].
The Dog-Leg Garden [1951] by Dorothea Street, a sister of the well-
known country writer A. G. Street, had an unusual setting and some
shrewd observation of child behaviour. Nora Lavrin and Molly Thorp
collaborated in a brilliantly realistic recreation of the Kentish scene,
The Hop Dog [1952], which was weakened by a clumsy intrusive plot.
Grace Hogarth, in *As a May Morning* [1958], captured the fleeting
beauty of adolescence. The first novel by Gillian Avery, *The Warden's
Niece* [1957], was full of promise; she was very much at home in
Victorian Oxford with a charming bluestocking heroine. Later stories
about the same characters have failed to maintain this high level.
Barbara Ker Wilson, however, improved on her interesting Victorian
story *Path-through-the-Woods* [1958] in a delightful romance of England
on the brink of the First World War *The Lovely Summer* [1960]. M. K.
Harris, in *Emily and the Headmistress* [1958] seemed, like so many of the
most promising new writers, more a writer about than for children.
Her insight into the bewildered mind of a small child left at school
during the holidays was unquestionably profound, but children who
were sufficiently mature to appreciate this were unlikely to be much
concerned over Emily's plight.

Halfway between the beginners and the veterans is Monica Edwards,
who after a commonplace start has written a series of intelligent studies
of country life and country folk. Her invention of plot is almost
invariably weak – *Cargo of Horses* [1951] was an exception – but
understanding of people and of the technique of country living enable
her to override this weakness.

A much less prolific writer, Antonia Forest, showed very little
weakness in her stories of the Marlow family. In *The Marlows and the
Traitor* [1953] and *Falconer's Lure* [1957] she showed extreme competence
in the marshalling of a complex plot, her writing was lucid, and her
eye for the idiosyncracies of character shrewd. These qualities were at
their highest in *End of Term* [1958], a story of boarding school life

which, in its concern for character and for moral values in a contemporary setting, claimed comparison with Elfrida Vipont.

A few writers showed some of Ransome's interest in the development of character or in practical activities in the open air. Of these Tyler Whittle chose one of Ransome's own settings in *Spades and Feathers* [1955], but, despite an expert's knowledge of birds, failed to match the master's sharp actuality. The veteran author, Roland Pertwee, wrote a splendid story about Devon, *The Islanders* in 1950, which had liveliness, some neat portraits of boys, a fairly satisfactory handling of ethical problems, and an engaging and youthful enthusiasm for the practical details of living wild. A sequel in the following year was disappointing. Richard Church, in *The Cave* [1950], had an important theme, the true nature of leadership, which would have appealed to Ransome, and an underground scene of the greatest interest; only a certain dullness in treatment kept this out of the highest class.

After nearly twenty years a sequel to *The Family from One End Street* appeared in 1956. *Further Adventures of the Family from One End Street* had in fact been for the most part written years before, but the manuscript had suffered many vicissitudes. When it at last appeared it was clear that Eve Garnett retained all her old magic. In the 'fifties, however, she was not alone in having an interest in working people. The poor, although no longer very poor, were fashionable. In 1958 E. W. Hildick started a series of stories written especially for the secondary modern boys of industrial England! Earlier A. Stephen Tring [Laurence Meynell] wrote an interesting book – *Barry's Exciting Year* [1951] – about a working-class boy experiencing the major crisis, educational and social, of the Eleven-Plus. (Elfrida Vipont's heroine in *The Spring of the Year* failed this test and was consigned to the Limbo of the Modern School – finding her soul in the experience). Ursula Moray Williams attempted a modern version of 'One End Street' in *The Binklebys at Home* [1951], going numerically better than Eve Garnett with ten little Binklebys and a plumber father, but achieving only a facile comedy. Alison Wright's *The Blakes* [1952], dealing with the acute contemporary problem of housing, was also unconvincing. John Griffiths' Welsh children in *Griff and Tommy* [1956] were more honest but lacked individuality. Elizabeth Stucley's *Magnolia Buildings* read like a sociologist's case-book. Much the best of these realistic stories were Leila Berg's *A Box for Benny* [1958] and Anne Barrett's *Songberd's Grove* [1957]. *Songberd's Grove* was a story of London streets and of Teddy Boys, sensible and competent if not profound Leila

Berg's story of a little Jewish boy was a *tour-de-force*, unerringly right
in observation, brimming with humanity and love.

It was in the 'fifties that Eleanor Estes' 'Moffat' stories came to
England. These gentle funny stories of a working-class family in a
small American town had much of Eve Garnett's clear sight and
affectionate humour in a setting which, for English readers, was both
strange and familiar.

William Mayne was not the only writer to pour new life into the
school-story. Geoffrey Trease's 'Bannermere' stories were more than
school-stories, but one of their chief excellences was the picture of
day-school boys and girls going about their daily business. His were
essentially contemporary stories. At the other extreme were Anthony
Buckeridge's enormously popular 'Jennings' stories, in the Greyfriars
tradition and, for all their 'modern' slang, as little concerned with
contemporary realities. These appealed by reason of naïve high spirits
and an infectious good humour.

There had been 'Career books' ever since *Ballet Shoes*, but it now
became a calculated policy of publishers to commission novels designed
to introduce young people to the hazards and rewards of various pro-
fessions. These were an interesting phenomenon of the 'fifties, although
it must be admitted that few individual 'Career Books' had much
interest. Most of the books on careers for girls concentrated on the
opportunities which the profession offered for courtship and marriage;
nearly all skipped lightly over the difficulties and setbacks encountered by their heroines. Hardly any had literary quality. For this
one had to turn to novels which were only incidentally career books,
like Richard Armstrong's *The Whinstone Drift* [1951], an adventure
story which showed a young man's attitude towards work in the
coalmines.

Only a few writers, mostly from overseas, chose to write about the
aftermath of war. Elizabeth Foreman Lewis wrote another of her moving stories of China in *To Beat a Tiger* [1957]; Meindert de Jong's
The House of Sixty Fathers [1958], apart from its contrived ending, had
greater power, pathos and an appealing wry humour. Margot Benary's
The Ark [1954] had an European setting, and she wrote with a quiet
eloquence of one aspect of the vast refugee problem. As a contribution
to the understanding of a great international problem, *The Ark* is
rivalled only by *The Silver Sword* [1956], in which Ian Serraillier brought
a poet's sensibility to a true story of a Polish family who, after the war,
searched through Europe for their lost parents. The story was written

without heroics, but the heroism and endurance of the children shone brightly in Serraillier's unobtrusively lovely prose.

(v) *Interpreting the Past*

The revolution in the writing of historical fiction, begun by Geoffrey Trease in the 'thirties, was completed in the 'fifties. At a time when a publisher, remembering his own boyhood, was reissuing Henty, Cynthia Harnett and Rosemary Sutcliff were recreating the past by infinitely different means. These two writers, alike only in excellence, were sharply contrasted in method.

Cynthia Harnett, who won the Carnegie Medal in 1951 with *The Wool-pack*, is a scholar and an artist who builds her story slowly from a multitude of tiny fragments of fact and conjecture. Every detail of her long complex stories has been verified by research in the study and on the ground. The drawings which illuminate the stories are as careful and authentic. It is remarkable that so little of the toil of construction shows in the result. The stories are not exciting, except in so far as all discovery is exciting, but they have an organic perfection derived from the author's genius for welding the many elements of her material with her own white-hot conviction. Her books are concerned to show something of the lives of ordinary people at important periods of the past. National events enter into the story only as they would have intruded into the lives of the common man. In *Ring Out Bow Bells* [1953] Agincourt is something that happened far away, but the return of Henry V in triumph to London is a pageant in which every Londoner has a part. In *The Load of Unicorn* [1959] Caxton is not the protagonist of a great intellectual revolution but a business man whose activities threaten vested interests in the City. The concern with everyday things give these books their remarkable intensity; their rare moments of revelation take them out of the sphere of scholarship into that of creation.

By contrast Rosemary Sutcliff is an intuitive historian. This is not to say that she is not most careful and exact in research, but that her ability to think herself back into the past transcends scholarship. Her acknowledged master is Kipling who had the same gift for feeling history through his nerves and seeking it through the soil. Rosemary Sutcliff began her career with *The Queen Elizabeth Story* [1950], a gentle, charmingly written story with an element of fantasy and a pervading sweetness which bordered on sentimentality. This was the vein of several succeeding stories until suddenly, in *Simon* [1953] the

author found her strength in a brilliant realistic picture of life in the
civil wars. In later books she has developed her gift for strong vigorous
narrative and replaced the sentimentality with an increasing harshness.
The Eagle of the Ninth [1954], a story of Roman rule in Britain, and
The Shield Ring [1956], which described the last stand of the Viking
settlers in the Lake District against the Normans, represent the finest
flower of her early maturity. In later stories, like *Warrior Scarlet* [1958]

a story of the Bronze Age, and *The Lantern Bearers*, a pendant to *The
Eagle of the Ninth*, describing the break-up of Roman Britain after the
departure of the Legions, with which Rosemary Sutcliff won the
Carnegie Medal in 1959, she has introduced difficult social and emotional motives which seem to threaten that she is ceasing to be a writer
for children; but in the splendidly Kiplingesque *Knight's Fee* [1960],
a story of England under William Rufus, she has returned to the powerful striding narrative of her finest manner.

Rosemary Sutcliff is one of the very few major writers to appear in
England since the war. She is a master of the declining art of story-
telling with an exact sense of timing, pace and invention. She has at
times shown a weakness for 'fine' writing which is her only sign of
immaturity. Her most remarkable quality is an ability to create
atmosphere, to let the reader see and hear and smell the past.

Only one other English historical novel has shown this quality.
Much highly competent work has been done, by Henry Treece in a
series of stories taking the history of Britain at times of crisis (the first

was *Legions of the Eagle* in 1954), by Ronald Welch in a number of stories which showed great mastery in the narrative of action and in knowledge of the technique of war, of which *Knight Crusader* won the Carnegie Medal in 1954, by Hilda Lewis [*The Gentle Falcon*, 1952], by Naomi Mitchison [*The Land the Ravens Found*, 1955], by Ursula Moray Williams [*Jockin the Jester*, 1951], by Rhoda Power [*Redcap Runs Away*, 1952], without any but the faintest gleam of that light which, in Rosemary Sutcliff's best work, gives the past a sudden radiance. The exception was *Ransom for a Knight* [1956], the only essay in historical fiction by Barbara Leonie Picard. This was the story of a Sussex girl whose father has been captured by the Scots at Bannockburn and who makes the journey from Lewes to pay his ransom. There may have been a basic improbability in the story, but the author's fine scrupulousness gave it an irresistible conviction, and her superb style, noble, flexible and timeless, made this an unforgettably moving story.

The only writer from overseas who has challenged these writers was Hans Baumann, a German who during the war had pondered certain historical truths and tried to put them into three books *Son of Columbus* [1957], *The Barque of the Brothers* [1958] and *The Sons of the Steppe* [1957]. These long complicated stories, full of difficult concepts and problems of psychology, are major works which are closer to Rosemary Sutcliff than to Cynthia Harnett, which are potentially far more significant than either but which are marred, at least in translation, by difficulties of communication. Even in *The Sons of the Steppe*, a story of the boyhood of Kublai Khan, which has the swiftest narrative, the problems of interpretation are man-size and defeat most child readers.

(vi) *The Best from Abroad*

Ever since *Emil* English editions of notable foreign books had been issued, but these were not considerable in numbers. In the 'fifties there was a spate of translations, particularly from the houses of Bodley Head, Methuen and University of London Press who made this an important aspect of their publishing policies. Not all these were of high quality, but at best the continental books opened new doors to English readers. There was a freedom from outworn traditions – or possibly an allegiance to unfamiliar traditions – which was refreshing.

Some of the continental writers were already familiar, like Erich Kastner and Marcel Aymé, but before 1952 few people had heard of René Guillot. The publication of *Companions of Fortune* in that year introduced a major writer. This complex, stormy, disturbing book, brilliantly translated by Geoffrey Trease, was something quite new. The tradition of the French corsairs was unfamiliar to English readers; so, largely, was the African setting. The characters were several sizes larger than life and their motives puzzling. The moral and philosophical ideas latent in the story were difficult to grasp. What made a complicated story deeply interesting was superb story-telling and masterly creation of atmosphere. The book breathed out the steamy heat of the African tropics. In the same year *Sama* showed René Guillot in a different light; the best jungle story since Kipling, it could not have been less like his work. There were, and continue to be, disturbing elements in Guillot's writing, but he stands head and shoulders above most of his contemporaries as narrator, adventurer and philosopher.

The renaissance of the French children's book has been one of the most interesting of post-war phenomena. Guillot is the most varied and prolific of a considerable band of writers. Of these Paul Berna has been outstandingly popular with English readers. *A Hundred Million Francs* [1957] was a story a little in the 'Emil' manner, dealing with the adventures of a gang of children in post-war Paris. It had pace, lively invention, and a shrewd understanding of child behaviour. Some of the same qualities appeared in Michel Bourguignon's *Line of Attack* [1959], one of the few books which showed understanding of the complexities of post-war child and adolescent psychology. M. A. Baudouy's *Children of the Marshes* [1958], beautifully evoking the atmosphere of Spain, was less accessible to children, and the same is even more true of Henri Bosco's books. It can hardly be doubted that *The Boy and the River* [1956] is one of the finest of the books of the 'fifties, but there is some doubt whether it is a book for children. In this and two sequels Bosco showed a profound understanding of children and of landscape. The lovely writing, in Gerard Hopkins' sensitive translation, had an almost hypnotic power. But only the most perceptive of children could enter this enchanted land.

The most interesting of the new German writers was Hans Baumann, whose best work was in the field of the historical novel. Max Voegeli's *The Wonderful Lamp* [1955] handled with great dexterity a complicated sprawling story in the 'Arabian Nights' manner. An equally complex, long, inimitable book was *Big Tiger and Christian* [1954], in which Fritz Muhlenweg followed the fortunes of two small boys in war-torn China. This was a book of heroic proportions, nobly developed and enlightened with gentle humour. Of several books from Holland the best was *Avalanche!*, by A. Rutgens van der Loeff [1957], a fine and highly readable story of adventure among neatly drawn characters and with a wise understanding of behaviour. This was, unlike some of the best of the continental books, completely accessible to English readers; so was the Swiss book *Timpetill* [1951] by Manfred Michael. This was the story of a Swiss town which the adult inhabitants, disgusted at the children's bad behaviour, abandoned. The way in which the children took over the management of their own affairs was described with great humour.

In some of the best of the American books, the writers looked to their European origins for inspiration. Far the most interesting of these was *The Wheel on the School* [1956] with which Meindert de Jong had won the Newbery Medal. This gentle picture of life in a Dutch village shone with truth and with a quiet unforced humour. Other Americans found material at home, like Lois Lenski in her charming *Strawberry Girl* [1951], another Newbery winner, Rutherford Montgomery in stories of wild life and animals like *Kildee House* [1953], and Kathrene Pinkerton in stories for older readers about the opening-up of Alaska. These showed a rare understanding of the minds of adolescent girls, as well as a gift for strong narrative. Two of the finest of all American books, looking back to the pioneering days, reached England in the 'fifties, long after their first editions. These were Laura Ingalls Wilder's *Little House in the Big Woods* [1956] and Elizabeth Coatsworth's *Away Goes Sally* [1955]. These were both stories of great sweetness and strength; Elizabeth Coatsworth's was enriched with the vision of a poet.

Two Australian writers gave some impression of the hard satisfying life of a country in which pioneering was still possible. M. E. Patchett, in *Ajax the Warrior* [1953], recalled the adventures of her own childhood, and Ray Harris, in *Turkey and Partners* [1954] wrote with artless sincerity of the everyday humours of a rural community; both of these books, excellent in many ways, lacked literary quality. Two fine books about Africa were of nearly the highest excellence in writing and in authenticity of reporting. These were by R. Forbes-Watson who in *Ambari* [1952] had one of the most brilliant and satisfying of first novels. This story of two little boys in Kenya and their adventures on and beside the sea moved briskly, had great humour and a quiet unobtrusive philosophy. "The time for school is when the tide is wrong for fishing" summed up neatly a universal truth of childhood. In *Shifta* [1954] Forbes-Watson changed his scene to Somaliland. This was a powerful, intensely serious story of life in the desert. It was full of violent action, of men fighting one another and the forces of nature.

It revealed, most miraculously, the beauty of this harsh country and the unstated love which it awakens in those who know it as their own. More almost than any other book of the century, *Shifta* enabled English children to see, with the eyes of the native, a land utterly alien to them and through those eyes to see its beauty and its wonder.

(vii) *New Lines of Enquiry*

The shadow of the school library lay heavily over the informational books of the 'fifties. Undoubtedly the existence of a large guaranteed market for competent work was an encouragement to publishers to venture on books and series which would have otherwise remained unwritten, and this was to the good. It is possible, however, that the school library was a reason for publishers playing safe, putting their resources into books for which there was a certain educational sale and leaving little room for the book of individual genius.

This meant more and more series. Many of these were excellent in conception, but only the rarest series maintained the highest standard in every title. The 'Young Traveller' books were particularly uneven in quality, admirable though the original idea was. R. J. Unstead's *Looking at History* was written in a lively style but was often guilty of over-simplification. Batsford's 'Junior Heritage' series were interesting because, resisting the temptation to water down their existing and most successful adult series, the publishers commissioned new work and showed, brilliantly, how photographs could be combined with art work in line and colour. Not all the 'Junior Heritage' books were equally good, but at their best, in, for example, Edmund Vale's *Churches* [1954], they showed the publisher in a challenging role. The Educational Supply Association's stories on similar subjects and Methuen's 'Outlines' were more conventionally educational in aim, and this showed itself in unimaginative formats.

This was particularly the age of the informational picture-book. First in the field were the Max Parrish 'Isotype' books edited by Marie Neurath, the earliest of which appeared soon after the war. These were clever simplifications of complex subjects, with a skilful use of diagrammatic devices in the manner devised by the Isotype Institute for illustrating statistical information during the war. They were designed for quite young children. The huge Rathbone books also looked like picture-books for the youngest with their 'Babar'-like format and brilliantly coloured pictures. Their content was much more difficult, although Lancelot Hogben's *Man Must Measure* [1955] and

Ronald Jessup's *Puzzle of the Past* [1956] achieved a most successful simplification of material. On the whole, however, such books were more interesting for their method than for their intrinsic quality.

Some of the series of 'Story biographies' begun after the war continued to keep a good standard. Maurice Collis's *Marco Polo* [1956] was an outstanding contribution to Faber's series, and two of Methuen's books by Jo Manton, *The Story of Albert Schweitzer* [1954] and *Portrait of Bach* [1957], proved brilliantly that a hero for children could be a man of peace. Collins' 'Brief Lives' were not written directly for children, but C. V. Wedgwood's *Montrose* had much to offer young readers. In a series of books from America, Elizabeth Ripley introduced the lives of great painters in alternate pages of text and reproduction, both of exceptional quality. The Oxford University Press, who sponsored these books, also published a series of biographies of explorers, some of them of no great interest, but Aubrey de Selincourt's *Nansen* told a great story in a manner not far short of inspiration. In Nansen's life children found courage "joined . . . with generosity and compassion", and De Selincourt in his quiet narrative missed no nuance of its greatness.

Among individual books of information, Edward Osmond's *A Valley Grows Up* won the Carnegie Medal for 1953. This was a study of history which had had its origin in a set of paintings by the author which had shown the changes in an imaginary valley over seventy centuries. These had been designed originally as educational wall-charts, but the author had been persuaded to provide a simple, fluent text. The result was an imaginative interpretation of history.

Two remarkable books attempted, in very different ways, to interpret religion to young readers. Pamela Whitlock's *The Open Book* [1956] was a thoughtful examination of the nature of faith. Elfrida Vipont had an even more ambitious aim in *The High Way* [1957]; this was an anthology of the spirit, with extracts from writers of all centuries. This was deeply interesting for its own quality and for the light it shed on the author's own work. There had been many attempts to retell the story of the Bible; perhaps the best of these was by Margherita Fanchiotti. She had written in 1953 a curiously convincing free treatment of the story of the Flood, *A Bow in the Clouds;* two years later her *Stories from the Bible* followed the narrative from the promise to Abraham to its fulfilment in Christ in a lovely timeless prose, intelligible and dignified. Of all the Bible story books this could be called worthy of its subject.

The 'fifties were particularly rich in anthologies of verse. Of these

James Reeves made a pleasantly lively collection with a wide age-interest in *The Merry-go-Round* [1955], and Pamela Whitlock's *All Day Long* [1954], which appealed mainly to older children, was especially rich in modern poems. Of special anthologies, there was a particular interest in Eve Garnett's *A Book of the Seasons* [1952]. This was a highly personal selection of poems (or fragments of poems) illustrating the seasons in England, and the compiler had added decorations in her finest manner to make a book of great beauty.

Since the first production of *Peter Pan* few dramatists had been concerned for the needs of children. In 1949 a writer of genius, Nicholas Stuart Gray, had produced his first play, and this, *Beauty and the Beast*, was published in 1951. A number of others followed year by year. Gray's lively invention and skill in the creation of atmosphere gave the most glowing life to the traditional tales, adding many characteristic details on the perimeter but never being untrue to the heart of the stories.

The two leading post-war poets continued to write, James Reeves achieving his best work in *The Blackbird in the Lilac* [1952]. In the same year Ian Serraillier's *The Ballad of the Kon-Tiki* offered a selection of fine verses in the mood of his previous manner, but three years later *Everest Climbed* marked a big stride forward, emotionally and stylistically. This was strong mature writing, in which Serraillier, purged of his early exuberance, had achieved a spare, hard eloquence.

Latest of the poets to turn to children's books was a veteran, Robert Graves. His collection of verses, *The Penny Fiddle* [1960], was strongly individual but, in its swift change of mood, in its wise simplicity, and in its effortless versatility of technique, this recalled across fifty years another collection of children's rhymes by a great poet, *Peacock Pie*. In this, as in so many other fields, the English literary tradition renewed itself.

(viii) *Illustrators Look Ahead*

Not all the illustrators of the 'fifties looked ahead. In 1952 B.B. (D. J. Watkins-Pitchford) brought out a fairy-book called *The Wind in the Wood* which looked directly back to the days of Rackham and Dulac. The superbly drawn colour-plates of 'The Nightingale' resembled those which Dulac had drawn forty years earlier even to the choice of subject and viewpoint. This artist more commonly works in scraper-board, a technique which, like the wood-engraving which it imitates, is temporarily out of favour for book-illustration. His precise line and scientifically accurate observation belong to the kind which Tunnicliffe was practising before the war. To this school, too, belongs Raymond Sheppard, whose drawings of animals are zoologically exact and strong in dramatic interest.

Among older artists Ernest H. Shepard, who had done little of interest in children's books since his Milne and Grahame days, made a return to his best style in two stories made from Eleanor Farjeon's plays. The line-drawings in *The Silver Curlew* [1953] were full of the humorous detail and invention which had made him the definitive illustrator of Milne; while falsifying nothing stated by the author, he added his own interpretation of the homely characters and their Norfolk homes in this most enchanting of stories.

The elegant mannered art of Pauline Diana Baynes belongs to a more leisured age than the 'fifties; she had affinities with Arthur Hughes, George Macdonald's illustrator, and it was inevitable that she should illustrate the neo-Macdonald 'Narnia' stories of C. S. Lewis. She was most successful in capturing the gentle fantasy of parts of these stories but she lacked both the robustness and the mysticism which the chronicles of Narnia often demanded. She was more at home with the delicate mock-scholarship of Tolkien's *Farmer Giles of Ham* [1949]. Her best work, very formal, highly civilised, but not too cold, went into Henri Pourrat's *A Treasury of French Tales* [1953] (not properly a children's book).

Of established artists the most prolific and consistently successful is Ardizzone. He has ranged wide, decorating James Reeves' nonsense verses and Eleanor Farjeon's evocative stories with equal sympathy and insight. He was in constant demand to illustrate the books of contemporary authors, but his greatest opportunity came with commissions for new drawings to two old books, one a major classic, the other a period piece. His drawings in line and colour for a new version, by James Reeves, of *Don Quixote* [1959] were full of vigour and penetrated deep into the heart of the story and the characters. An attempt by the Oxford University Press to introduce Surtees to children [*Hunting with Mr. Jorrocks*, 1956], was not entirely successful, but Ardizzone's illustrations were in his happiest vein and showed that he was by no means inferior to Leech. Except in his own 'Little Tim' books he has always seemed most at home with line, but the colour plates of Mr. Jorrocks and his friends were happy in their Victorian manner, with a conscious but not tiresome archaism.

Among Ardizzone's contemporaries, only Joan Kiddell-Monroe has equalled him in versatility and in output. Her most characteristic work is in the beautifully designed decorations to the Oxford 'Fairy Tales and Legends' series, but she has also shown a lively sense of humour, notably in Lorna Wood's 'Hag' books. Robin Jacques, her equal in elegance and in a sense of design, is much less prolific. Each of his books is a major event, but he has done nothing better than the fine line-drawings in the *Collected Stories for Children* of Walter de la Mare [1957] which, for all their artifice, emphasised the homeliness of De la Mare's world. Another experienced illustrator, Richard Kennedy, has done much work which was competent but undistinguished; at his best, in Eleanor Farjeon's *Martin Pippin in the Apple Orchard* [1952], lyrical and almost ecstatic, or *Timpetill* [1951], richly humane, absorbed in the atmosphere and the topography of his scene, he stepped into the front rank of modern illustrators. C. Walter Hodges had done his most imaginative work before the war, but his drawings for Rosemary Sutcliff's earliest books and William Mayne's 'Choir School' stories were exquisitely drawn and accurate in detail.

Most distinguished work was done in the 'fifties by Lynton Lamb, a restrained and evocative artist whose delicate line-drawings were the perfect accompaniment of Henri Bosco's sad haunted tales, but who was a little less successful as an illustrator to William Mayne.

The most exciting work of a new artist in the 'fifties was by William Stobbs. The power of his portrait-drawings in historical stories by Donald Welch and adventure-stories by Ronald Syme distracted attention from his fine sensibility and the careful research which went into every detail of his work. His success in history and adventure made him a 'typed' artist, but he escaped this fate in the brilliant colour of *Kashtanka* and the poetical insight of *A Bundle of Ballads* [both 1959]. Stobbs' professional knowledge of typography helps him in the integration of text and picture. Peggy Fortnum's work provides a strange contrast to Stobbs' dynamic drawing. In swift, fluid line she has captured the sweetness of Diana Ross's Miss Pussy or the farcical humour of Michael Bond's Paddington. In her decorations for Eleanor Farjeon's verses, *The Children's Bells*, she found a graphic parallel to the poet's effortless lyricism.

In 1950 there were comparatively few illustrators doing work of quality in England. By 1960, through the enterprise of publishers like the Oxford University Press, Bodley Head and Constable, a new generation of illustrators had changed the face of the English children's book. Not all the new work pleased the critics or the children; there could be no question of the technical excellence or the artistic integrity of these young illustrators, who boldly explored the scenery, the characters and the ideas of their authors. These artists did not constitute a 'school'; their backgrounds and training differed widely and strong individuality prevented them from yielding to influences. What is common to the work of such artists as Margery Gill, Geraldine Spence and Don Higgins is fine draughtsmanship, intelligence and insight; youth is clearly a characteristic of each.

Outstanding among the achievements of the new generation of illustrators were the drawings for *Tom's Midnight Garden*, *The Lantern Bearers*, and *Tangara*. Susan Einzig caught precisely the atmosphere of Philippa Pearce's ghost-story, with the strange actuality of its Victorian

sequences and the harshness of the present. Susan Einzig, a German artist trained and now living in England, used no tricks of style in this book; she simply thought herself into the story. Charles Keeping has a more aggressive style. For Rosemary Sutcliff's medal-winning book he provided heavy stylised drawings which, without conscious archaism, conveyed a feeling of the remote past. His art accepts easily the conventions of the book, and his bold designs in *The Lantern Bearer* are an organic part of the pages on which they grow. Some adult readers found them disturbing (which they were intended to be); to many children the massive strength of Keeping's warriors seemed a proper accompaniment to Rosemary Sutcliff's heroic narrative. Brian Wildsmith is the most difficult of the young illustrators, and he was never more difficult than in Nan Chauncy's *Tangara*. There is no facile charm in these elusive designs, but they belong to the story, capturing its atmosphere and matching the drama of its crises. Such drawings seem to have been wrung from the artist, so painfully have the lines been drawn; but in his anguish Brian Wildsmith has felt the strength and the grief of this great story. His illustrations, difficult as they are, are definitive; it is impossible to think of the book without them.

It is a far cry from Brian Wildsmith to H. R. Millar, whose drawings for E. Nesbit's stories seemed perhaps as strange to the Edwardian reader as Wildsmith's seem today. In technique and in inspiration the two artists are profoundly different. Both, however, belong to the English tradition; and, if it seems perverse to find a traditional element in Wildsmith, it is worth remembering that Samuel Palmer is a part of that tradition. In Wildsmith's mysticism, in his search for light through darkness, there is something of the youthful Palmer.

AN APOLOGY

Twice a year *The Times Literary Supplement* produces a special Children's Book Section. In this admittedly hasty glance at contemporary children's literature, rather more words are printed, in each issue, than I have used in attempting a survey of sixty years of modern children's books. It has been difficult to prevent the book becoming a book-list. Even so, I have had to leave out mention of many books which have given me genuine pleasure. In seeking to trace important trends in writing for children I have necessarily, and reluctantly, failed to mention many writers who have something to say and who say it effectively.

I therefore offer sincere apologies to those writers whose names do not appear in these pages. Children's literature is in a healthy state in 1962. This is due not only to the Maynes and the Pearces and the Sutcliffs, who would be outstanding in any age, but also to the amazingly high general standard. It is tempting to say that there are no bad books, as there are no plain girls, today. This is not true. What is true is that children have never, in their own homes or in the school and public library, had a better chance of finding, wherever their choice falls, books which have style, intelligence and an original viewpoint. It is no bad thing to be a child in the 'sixties.

READING LIST

General

DARTON, F. J. HARVEY
Children's books in Britain: five centuries of social life. Cambridge University Press, 1932. Second edition, 1958.

Although this book does not cover the twentieth century, it is essential reading for all students of modern children's books.

EYRE, FRANK
20th century children's books. British Council (Longmans Green), 1952.

FORD, BORIS, *ed.*
Young writers, young readers. Hutchinson, 1960.

Contains critical articles on children's writers originally published in *The Journal of Education.*

GREEN, ROGER LANCELYN
Tellers of tales. Enlarged edition. Edward Ward, 1953.
Biographical and appreciative studies written for young people.

HAZARD, PAUL
Les livres, les enfants et les hommes. Paris, Boivin, 1932, translated as Books, children and men. Boston, Horn Book, 1944.

HORN BOOK MAGAZINE
A 'Horn Book' sampler on children's books and reading; edited by Norma R. Fryatt. Boston, Horn Book, 1959.
A selection of articles originally published in *Horn Book.*

HÜRLIMANN, BETTINA
Europäische Kinderbücher in drei Jahrhunderten. Zurich, Atlantis, 1959.

ILLUSTRATORS OF CHILDREN'S BOOKS, 1744–1945; compiled by Bertha E. Mahoney, Louise Payson Latimer and Beulah Folmsbee. Boston, Horn Book, 1947.

ILLUSTRATORS OF CHILDREN'S BOOKS, 1946–1956; compiled by Ruth Hill Viguers, Marcia Dalphin and Bertha Mahoney Miller. Boston, Horn Book, 1958.

KERLAN, IRVIN
Newbery and Caldecott awards: a bibliography of first editions. Minneapolis, University of Minnesota Press, 1949.

Kunitz, Stanley J., and Haycroft, Howard, *eds.*
>The junior book of authors. N.Y., H. W. Wilson, 1934. Second edition, revised, 1951.
>
>Biographical articles, mostly about American writers and based on information supplied by the writers.

The Library Association
>Chosen for children; an account of the books which have been awarded the Library Association Carnegie Medal, 1936–1957. Library Association, 1957.

The Library Association. Youth Libraries Section.
>Children's books of this century. A first list of books covering the years 1899 to 1956 chosen for the library of children's literature now being formed at Chaucer House. 1958.

Meigs, Cornelia, *and others*
>A critical history of children's literature. New York, Macmillan, 1953.
>
>The only book which includes consideration at length of children's books of the twentieth century. American bias.

Miller, Bertha Mahoney, and Field, Elinor Whitney, *eds.*
>Newbery Medal books: 1922–1955, with their authors' acceptance papers and related papers and related material chiefly from the Horn Book Magazine. Horn Book papers, Volume I. Boston, Horn Book, 1955.

— Caldecott Medal books: 1938–1957, with the artists' acceptance papers and related materials chiefly from the Horn Book Magazine. Horn Book Papers, Volume II. Boston, Horn Book, 1957.

Moore, Anne Carroll
>My roads to childhood. New York, Doubleday, 1939
>A collection of critical writing.

Moore, Anne Carroll, *ed.*
>The three owls: a book about children's books, their authors and critics. New York, Macmillan, 1925

— The three owls; second book. New York, Coward McCann, 1928.

— The three owls; third book. New York, Coward McCann, 1931.
>Reviews, many of them by the editor.

Morris, Charles H.
>The illustration of children's books. Library Association, 1957.
>Library Association pamphlet No. 16.

New York Public Library
>Reading without boundaries, essays presented to Anne Carroll

Moore on the occasion of the fiftieth anniversary of the inaugura-
tion of library service to children at the New York Public Library.
Edited by Frances Lander Spain. New York, Public Library, 1956.

RYDER, JOHN
Artists of a certain line. A selection of illustrators for children's
books. Bodley Head, 1960.

SMITH, JANET ADAM
Children's illustrated books. Collins, 1948.
'Britain in Pictures' series.

SMITH, LILLIAN H.
The unreluctant years. A critical approach to children's literature.
Chicago, American Library Association, 1953.

TREASE, GEOFFREY
Enjoying books. Phoenix House, 1951.
Written for children.

— Tales out of school. Heinemann, 1948.

WHITE, DOROTHY NEAL
About books for children. Oxford University Press, 1946.

WHITE, DOROTHY [NEAL]
Books before five. New Zealand Council of Educational Research,
1954.
An examination, in journal form, of the reaction of the author's daughter to
the stories read to her.

Books on Individual Writers and Illustrators

Barrie, Sir James Matthew
ASQUITH, *Lady* CYNTHIA
Portrait of Barrie. Barrie, 1954.

GREEN, ROGER LANCELYN
J. M. Barrie (a Bodley Head Monograph). Bodley Head, 1960.

De la Mare, Walter
BRAIN, *Sir* W. RUSSELL
Tea with Walter de la Mare. Faber, 1957.

CLARK, LEONARD
Walter de la Mare (a Bodley Head Monograph). Bodley Head,
1960.

HOPKINS, KENNETH
Walter de la Mare. British Council (Longmans), 1953.

NATIONAL BOOK LEAGUE
Walter de la Mare: a checklist. Cambridge University Press, 1956.
REID, FORREST
Walter de la Mare. A critical study. Faber, 1929.
TRIBUTES TO WALTER DE LA MARE ON HIS SEVENTY-FIFTH BIRTHDAY.
Faber, 1948

Edwards, Monica
EDWARDS, MONICA
The unsought farm. Michael Joseph, 1954.

Farjeon, Eleanor
COLWELL, EILEEN H.
Eleanor Farjeon (a Bodley Head Monograph). Bodley Head, 1961.
FARJEON, ELEANOR
A nursery in the 'nineties. Gollancz, 1935.
New edition. Oxford University Press, 1960.

Gibbings, Robert
GIBBINGS, ROBERT
The wood engravings of Robert Gibbings. Art and Technics, 1949.
—— The wood engravings of Robert Gibbings. Dent, 1959.

Grahame, Kenneth
CHALMERS, PATRICK
Kenneth Grahame: life, letters and unpublished work. Methuen,
1933.
GRAHAME, KENNETH
First whisper of 'The Wind in the Willows'. Edited . . . by Elspeth
Grahame. Methuen, 1944.
GREEN, PETER
Kenneth Grahame, 1859–1932. Murray, [1959].

Kipling, Rudyard
BROWN, HILTON
Rudyard Kipling: a new appreciation. Hamish Hamilton, 1945.
CARRINGTON, CHARLES
Rudyard Kipling; his life and work. Macmillan, 1955.
STEWART, J. M.
Rudyard Kipling: a bibliographical catalogue, edited by A. W.
Yeats. Toronto, Dalhousie University Press, 1959.

SUTCLIFF, ROSEMARY
   Rudyard Kipling (a Bodley Head Monograph). Bodley Head,
   1960.
TOMPKINS, J. M. S.
   The art of Rudyard Kipling. Methuen, 1959.

Lynch, Patricia
LYNCH, PATRICIA
   A storyteller's childhood. Dent, 1947

Masefield, John
HANDLEY-TAYLOR, GEOFFREY, *ed.*
   John Masefield, O.M.: a bibliography. Cranbrook Town Press,
   [1960].
SPARK, M.
   John Masefield. Nevill, 1953.

Mee, Arthur
HAMMERTON, *Sir* JOHN
   Child of wonder. An intimate biography of Arthur Mee. Hodder
   and Stoughton, 1946.

Milne, A. A.
MILNE, A. A.
   It's too late now: the autobiography of a writer. Methuen, 1939.

Nesbit, E.
BELL, ANTHEA
   E. Nesbit (a Bodley Head Monograph). Bodley Head, 1960.
MOORE, DORIS LANGLEY
   E. Nesbit. A biography. Benn, 1933
STREATFEILD, NOEL
   Magic and the magician. E. Nesbit and her children's books.
   Benn, 1958.

Potter, Beatrix
CROUCH, MARCUS
   Beatrix Potter (a Bodley Head Monograph). Bodley Head, 1960.
LANE, MARGARET
   The tale of Beatrix Potter. A biography. Warne, 1946.
POTTER, BEATRIX
   The art of Beatrix Potter. Warne, [1955].

QUINBY, JANE
Beatrix Potter: a bibliographical check-list. New York, 1954.

Rackham, Arthur
HUDSON, DEREK
Arthur Rackham, his life and work. Heinemann, 1960.

Ransome, Arthur
SHELLEY, HUGH
Arthur Ransome (a Bodley Head Monograph). Bodley Head, 1960.

Shepard, Ernest H.
SHEPARD, ERNEST H.
Drawn from memory. Methuen, 1957.

Streatfeild, Noel
WILSON, BARBARA KER
Noel Streatfeild (a Bodley Head Monograph). Bodley Head, 1961.

Trease, Geoffrey
MEEK, MARGARET
Geoffrey Trease (a Bodley Head Monograph). Bodley Head, 1960.

Whistler, Rex
WHISTLER, LAURENCE
Rex Whistler, 1905–1944: his life and his drawings. Art and Technics, 1948.
WHISTLER, LAURENCE, and FULLER, RONALD
The work of Rex Whistler. Batsford, 1960.

Booklists

(From the great number of published booklists on this subject, two only have been included because they are outstandingly authoritative.)

LINES, KATHLEEN M., *ed.*
Four to fourteen: a library of books for children. Second edition. National Book League (Cambridge University Press), 1956.
THOMSON, JEAN, *ed.*
Books for boys and girls. Third edition. Toronto, Ryerson Press, 1954.
— A supplement, 1953–1958. Toronto, Ryerson Press, 1960.

APPENDIX

THE LIBRARY ASSOCIATION CARNEGIE MEDAL

The Library Association Carnegie Medal is awarded annually for an outstanding book for children by a British subject, published during the preceding year.

At the end of each year recommendations for the award are invited from members of the Library Association, who are asked to submit a preliminary list of not more than three titles from which the Committee makes a final selection.

The award is open to works of non-fiction as well as fiction and the choice is based upon consideration of all the following points:

FICTION. (i) Plot; (ii) Style; (iii) Characterization; (iv) Format (including production and illustrations, if any).

NON-FICTION. (i) Accuracy; (ii) Method of presentation; (iii) Style; (iv) Format, etc.

The following is a list of L.A. Carnegie Medal winners since the institution of the award.

LIST OF LIBRARY ASSOCIATION CARNEGIE MEDAL WINNERS

1936 RANSOME, Arthur. *Pigeon post* (Cape.)
1937 GARNETT, Eve. *The family from One End Street* (Muller).
1938 STREATFEILD, Noel. *The circus is coming* (Dent).
1939 DOORLY, Eleanor. *Radium woman* (Heinemann).
1940 BARNE, Kitty. *Visitors from London* (Dent).
1941 TREADGOLD, M. *We couldn't leave Dinah* (Cape).
1942 "B.B." (D. J. WATKINS-PITCHFORD). *The little grey men* (Eyre & Spottiswoode).
1943 Prize withheld as no book considered suitable.
1944 LINKLATER, Eric. *The wind on the moon* (Macmillan).
1945 Prize withheld as no book considered suitable.
1946 GOUDGE, Elizabeth. *The little white horse* (Univ. London Press).
1947 DE LA MARE, Walter. *Collected stories for children* (Faber).
1948 ARMSTRONG, R. *Sea change* (Dent.)
1949 ALLEN, Agnes. *The story of your home* (Faber).
1950 FOULDS, Elfrida Vipont. *The lark on the wing* (O.U.P.).
1951 HARNETT, Cynthia. *The wool-pack* (Methuen).

1952 NORTON, Mary. *The borrowers* (Dent).
1953 OSMOND, Edward. *A valley grows up* (O.U.P.).
1954 FELTON, Ronald Oliver ("Ronald Welch"). *Knight Crusader* (O.U.P.).
1955 FARJEON, Eleanor. *The little bookroom* (O.U.P.).
1956 LEWIS, C. S. *The last battle* (Bodley Head).
1957 MAYNE, W. *A grass rope* (O.U.P.).
1958 PEARCE, Ann Philippa. *Tom's midnight garden* (O.U.P.).
1959 SUTCLIFF, Rosemary. *The lantern bearers* (O.U.P.).
1960 CORNWALL, I. W. *The making of man* (Phoenix House).

KATE GREENAWAY MEDAL

The Library Association Kate Greenaway Medal is intended to recognize the importance of illustrations in children's books. It is awarded to the artist who, in the opinion of the Library Association, has produced the most distinguished work in the illustration of children's books during the preceding year.

The artist must be a British subject and the work published in the United Kingdom.

Books intended for older as well as younger children are included, and reproduction will be taken into account.

Recommendations for the award are invited from members of the L.A. who are asked to submit a preliminary list of not more than three titles.

1955 Prize withheld as no book considered suitable.
1956 ARDIZZONE, Edward. *Tim all alone* (O.U.P.).
1957 DRUMMOND, V. H. *Mrs. Easter and the storks* (Faber).
1958 Prize withheld as no book considered suitable.
1959 STOBBS, W. *Kashtanka* and *A bundle of ballads* (O.U.P.).
1960 ROSE, Gerald. *Old Winkle and the seagulls* (Faber).

INDEX